Dramatherapy

Developing emotional stability

Penny McFarlane

David Fulton Publishers

David Fulton Publishers Ltd
The Chiswick Centre, 414 Chiswick High Road, London W4 5TF

www.fultonpublishers.co.uk

First published in Great Britain in 2005 by David Fulton Publishers.

10 9 8 7 6 5 4 3 2 1

David Fulton Publishers is a division of Granada Learning Limited, part of ITV plc.

British Library Cataloguing in Publication Data
A catalogue record for this book is available from the British Library.

ISBN 1–84312–265–0

Typeset by FiSH Books, London
Printed and bound in Great Britain by Ashford Colour Press

To the courage and resilience of all children everywhere and to the magical child in all of us.

The writing of this book has been a source both of great enjoyment and soul-searching for me and I offer it not as a definitive answer but rather as a way of working which I have found to be of benefit to troubled children. In these days of quantitative analysis my admiration and appreciation go out to those who have put faith and trust in this qualitative approach. Perhaps we do not need to know all the answers or make it all add up: for then, like the child, we can find a room within ourselves where magic can happen.

Contents

The Stories

Acknowledgements

Above all I am grateful to Sylvia Wheadon whose faith in me and my work has supported me throughout the years and in the writing of this book: likewise to Annie Tempest for her support and encouragement as a friend and in her capacity as Head Teacher and Associate Member of the DfES. My thanks also go to Vicky Coxon, Jack Griffiths and Steve Soames whose initial risk-taking and enthusiasm for this way of working has, I hope, paid off. I would also like to acknowledge the care and commitment shown by the primary and secondary school staff with whom I have come into contact. Their willingness to engage with my work in spite of their heavy schedules has always been a source of admiration and amazement to me. To my friends (they know who they are) who have encouraged and listened to me (and in the case of Carol offered me hospitality) I offer my heartfelt appreciation and a promise that I will talk about something else now! Finally, the ongoing interest and support of my husband Stuart and my children Leonie and Alexine has made the writing of this book possible – to them, as ever, my love and thanks.

Foreword

Penny McFarlane's career in the field of primary and secondary education began 25 years ago. After many years of teaching, Penny qualified as a dramatherapist, finding the combination of teaching and dramatherapy a valuable way of working with children with special needs, which, in turn, inspired the writing of this book, written as it is in a very user-friendly language.

Penny's work as the Coordinator of a Creative Arts Therapy project in schools in an inner-city area is well known to me and it gives me great pleasure to recommend her work to others. I believe it to be at the forefront of the latest thinking in educational development in schools, and to be in line with government legislation, including, most recently, the 2004 Children's Bill, which urges all adults to work together in partnership to better meet the needs of the child.

The book contains an insight into the magical Rainbow Room where Penny enables the child to think about and connect with their feelings by exploring their dreams, creating stories, and by using puppets and pre-written material such as fairy tales. In this way the children can not only have their own stories witnessed but are also able to express their fears, sorrows and joys, and are able to process the feeling to the point of resolution.

The stories, as well as the exercises and ideas, can be used as a practical guide to anyone whose life or professional work brings them into contact with children. It is particularly useful when working with children who may be experiencing emotional difficulties and who need additional support at home or in the classroom.

Sylvia Wheadon
Educational Trainer, Dramatherapist, Psychodramatist/Psychotherapist

Preface

The inspiration for this book grew out of my work as a dramatherapist in an inner-city primary school and the stories that the children shared with me in the Rainbow Room.

For 15 years I had been a teacher both in primary and secondary education, and I had always been moved by the ability of many children to rise above their current difficulties and face life. It was not how badly behaved they were that interested me but how well they coped given the scope and depth of their problems.

I felt that through their behaviour they were trying to tell me something, and training as a dramatherapist gave me the opportunity to endeavour to understand and interpret their behaviour.

At first, after qualifying, I worked in various primary and secondary schools on a peripatetic basis, offering one-to-one and group sessions. In January 2001 I was offered a post as a dramatherapist in a primary school in a deprived inner-city area as part of a research project into the effectiveness of early psychodynamic intervention in the raising of emotional literacy and self-esteem with children who were at risk of exclusion. The project went well and expanded to include the introduction of other arts therapists into interested schools.

The aim of this book is not to produce a handbook for using dramatherapy in schools; for that, a registered course in dramatherapy training would need to be undertaken (details on courses and where to obtain more information is given in Appendix B). Instead, the intention here is to provide an interesting and enlightening introduction to this type of therapeutic intervention along with some suggestions for exercises and activities to help a troubled child in the absence of a trained therapist. It goes without saying that specialist help should always be brought in if the issues are such that the member of staff feels out of their depth. Furthermore, it is strongly advised that any adult undertaking work of this kind with a troubled child first undergoes a training in as many as possible of the available courses as mentioned in Appendix B and also undergoes some form of supervision.

For the purposes of confidentiality all the names of the children have been changed and, where appropriate, significant details in their backgrounds have been altered to preserve anonymity. Wherever possible the permission of the children and their carers to use their stories has been sought and for this my grateful thanks goes out to them.

Chapters 1 to 4 are intended as an introduction to dramatherapy including an explanation of the therapeutic value of telling your own story and the significance of metaphor. Subsequent chapters deal with specific issues such as the use of pre-written material, recurrent themes, dream work, bereavement and group work. Each chapter carries a summary and, if applicable, ideas for working in a simple, safe way along these lines. When, to illustrate a particular point, an allusion is made to a child and their story in the preceding and subsequent chapters, that story and the child's background is included in the story section of the book.

The stories themselves come from the heart and as such deserve to stand alone in their simplicity. For this reason a detailed exploration into their possible meanings has been purposely omitted. It is hoped that, for those reading this book, the stories will provide, in a way which no amount of academic reading can, a sense not only of how dramatherapy can work, but also of the numinous essence of a child's mind and the value and magic of play.

To avoid confusion the child is referred to as 'he' and the therapist as 'she'.

Chapter 1

An Introduction to Dramatherapy

The play's the thing/Wherein I'll catch the conscience of the King.
(*Hamlet,* William Shakespeare)

What is dramatherapy?

The British Association of Dramatherapists has given its definition of dramatherapy as having as its main focus the 'intentional use of the healing aspects of drama and theatre as the therapeutic process.' It further explains that dramatherapy is 'a method of working and playing which uses action methods to facilitate creativity, imagination, learning, insight and growth' (see Appendix B). This chapter will explore the ways in which dramatherapy, through cultivating a safe trusting environment, can employ creative methods to bring about positive change for the child.

Many people ask about the difference between drama and dramatherapy since in the hands of a good drama teacher, therapy in the form of raised self-esteem, self-confidence and empowerment often takes place anyway. The difference lies in the word 'intentional' in that dramatherapy may be said to be the intentional use of drama for therapeutic ends. Similar techniques may be employed but for a different reason. The means may be the same but the intended end or outcome is different.

So what are these techniques? They will vary depending on the client or child and the issues involved. They may entail movement or voice or both, improvisation and role play, story making and story telling or more specialised techniques such as sculpting, mirroring or role reversal. They may involve the use of clay or paint, masks and puppets, material, costumes and props – or they may simply rely upon the dramatic use of the therapeutic relationship between therapist and child.

The therapeutic relationship

Much time is spent in creating this necessary relationship before the work actually starts. According to Axline (1989) the most important element in the session is the relationship between the child and the therapist. There must be a necessary acceptance of the child as he is, a witnessing of what the child has to offer and a reflecting back of the child's feelings, emotions and situation. In this way the therapist can be emotionally present for that child.

Winnicott (1965) claims that the therapeutic relationship has much in common with the natural processes of the mother–infant relationship in that they share the underlying principles of tolerance, acceptance and respect, being the attributes of the good-enough mother. The child must learn to trust the therapist as one who will provide them with the opportunities to heal and change in much the same way as the therapist must trust in the child's ability to make the necessary changes in his life if given the opportunity.

The issue of trust

The space

The issue of trust is a major consideration in any dramatherapeutic engagement. In order to create a space in which the child feels safe enough to explore their feelings several points need to be taken into consideration. There is first the practical interpretation of the word 'space'. A busy corridor is simply not conducive to work of this kind. Far better to use the cluttered Maths cupboard where at least privacy is guaranteed and the child has the security of having four walls around them. Likewise, a huge hall, while possible for some group work, is not recommended for the more fragile structure of the one-to-one session. In creating the 'Rainbow Room' from the landing area of a disused fire escape in an inner-city primary school, the aim was to provide a space which resembled as near as possible the original place of safety for the child – namely, the womb.

It is equally important that this space, once created and established as the place of safety where feelings may be unravelled and change may happen, does not in itself change. There is sometimes a tendency in schools to determine the importance of an activity by the numbers of people taking part. Hence the dramatherapist and child may well find themselves moved around from week to week depending on the number of other engagements in the school diary. It is therefore vital that a space is found (or created!) which can remain at the disposal of the dramatherapist come what may. A change of space may mean not only that any important work done so far may have to begin again, but also that an element of doubt may creep in on the part of the child about whether this person can provide what the child is beginning to hope and trust they can – a consistently secure and accepting environment.

The contract

The fabric of the trusting relationship is as fragile as it is important. Many children who come for therapy will not have had positive experiences of being able to trust. The drawing up of some sort of contract between the therapist and child may help to place the relationship on a firmer footing. It is helpful if the ideas for the contract can be elicited as far as possible from the child. The therapist may like to use a metaphor such as that of baking a cake, as described in Diana's story 'Through the Wall', in order to make the idea more accessible to the child.

However it is accomplished, the issue of how long the contract will run is of primary concern. The child needs to know that there will not be a sudden ending to this new-found relationship. Equally, however, the child needs to be given the opportunity to put into the contract what they feel will help make it work. In Diana's case, this was 'behaviour and stuff'. By being given the opportunity to contribute to the contract the child becomes the co-creator in the 'play' – a co-facilitator in the therapeutic scenario rather than someone that therapy is being 'done to'. This concept of joint ownership of a session and of letting the child take the lead will be discussed in Chapter 3.

Confidentiality

Hand in hand with the idea of a contract is the issue of confidentiality. The child needs to be able to trust that the therapist is able to hold and keep safe anything which he divulges. At the same time, the therapist needs to work with the teacher, teaching assistants and special educational needs coordinator (SENCO), who have possibly referred the child as a result of their concerns. Due to the way in which dramatherapy works with metaphor, the issue will very often remain within the metaphor and no allusion need be made as to its connection to the child's reality. This is discussed further in Chapter 3.

Confidentiality is a thin dividing line which needs to be trodden and the good of the child must always be the primary motive. In general, the way I work is to explain to the child that I am working with whoever referred them – teacher, head teacher, SENCO – and that we are all concerned as to their happiness. In accordance with Child Protection there must obviously be some statement to the effect that a referral would have to be made if it was thought the child were in danger. Thereafter, it is the process of the child and not the content of the sessions which may be discussed on a confidential basis if it is felt to be beneficial to the child.

Dramatic distancing

Once an atmosphere of trust has been created, the modus operandi of dramatherapy can come into play. One of the main principles of dramatherapy centres on the use of fiction to express a truth. The age-old story of the man who goes to the doctor to confide an embarrassing problem which he attributes to his friend serves as an analogy here. 'Doctor, Doctor, I've a friend who...' creates the safety net which the man needs to express that which he finds inexpressible.

By creating an 'as if' scenario the situation may be considered from an objective and not a subjective viewpoint, thus allowing the emotions involved to be distanced until such time as the psyche feels that it is safe enough to engage with them. As Jennings (1990: 6) explains, 'Paradoxically this distance enables us to come closer and to experience at a greater depth.'

Thus, dramatic distancing, brought about through, for example, the use of projection or role play with the help of masks, puppets and small figures or objects, can bring about a 'space' where emotions can be expressed and explored and healing can take place. In this way, the dramatic space and the therapeutic space are very closely linked. The emotions expressed may have to do with personal issues or they may be concerned on a broader spectrum with more social or religious matters.

The objectives

Whatever the issues, the objectives of dramatherapy are to use the psychological processes of creativity and learning, spontaneity, play and imagination to focus on the positive, to build positive relationships, to raise self-esteem and to promote personal development and growth, outcomes which are in close alignment with the holistic approach of the 2004 Children's Act.

Summary

- Dramatherapy differs from drama in that it is the *intentional* use of drama for therapeutic ends.

- Dramatherapy involves a variety of techniques and props similar to those used in drama.

- The therapeutic relationship between therapist and child is a primary consideration.

- Trust is a key element of this relationship.

- Trust can be enhanced by use of an appropriate space and by the drawing up of a contract.

- Confidentiality often remains within the metaphor. It centres on the process of the child and not the content of the sessions.

- Dramatic distancing further enhances the atmosphere of safety.

- The objectives of dramatherapy emphasise the building blocks of positive growth in accordance with the latest holistic approach to educational thinking.

Chapter 2
A Way of Working
Embodiment–projection–role

You can discover more about a person in an hour of play than in a year of conversation. (Plato)

Embodiment–projection–role

An important theory central to the process of dramatherapy is that of embodiment, projection and role. To enter into a brief explanation of this theory is to provide a useful framework for explaining the methodology used by many dramatherapists. There are other models of dramatherapy including Meldrum's Theatrical Model and Landy's Role Model but the Creative Expressive Model as promoted by Sue Jennings employs the embodiment–projection–role process and is the one I have found most useful in my work.

Embodiment

The embodiment–projection–role process corresponds in a general way to the stages of child development as outlined by the psychological theorists J. Piaget and E. H. Erikson. During the first couple of years the child is concerned primarily with bodily sensations, with chewing, sucking, tasting and feeling. This is Piaget's 'motory/sensory developmental stage' and Erikson's 'trust versus mistrust'. The ideas of Erikson are useful to a dramatherapist since they emphasise the areas of dramatic conflict which can arise if these stages are not progressed through normally (see Appendix B).

The importance of the trusting relationship between therapist and child has already been discussed in Chapter 1 and it is worth noting that many sessions often begin with some embodiment work before progressing to the projection and role stages. In my own work I find it useful to begin by playing with tactile objects such as slime balls, or soft, brightly coloured material, as this grounds and anchors the child in a non-threatening way in the involvement of the session.

The embodiment stage is a very important time for the child since it is when he first becomes aware of self. Some children who, for some reason, have not explored this phase sufficiently remain stuck at this stage and it is important to allow them time to rediscover the joy of this form of self-exploration while providing enough opportunities for them to progress to the next stage. Children who have suffered neglect or abuse will sometimes go backwards and forwards between stages, and it is important to let the child lead, following with suggestions of ways in which the child might explore that particular phase. This phase is all about the child becoming aware of their own body, acknowledging and, if possible, externalising the feelings. So it was with Alexa before she told her stories of 'The Children's Island', 'Fuzz the Bear' and 'The Dancing Butterfly'. Making the anger mountain and drawing out her feelings enabled her to focus upon the way her body was feeling. Only when this had been done was she ready to move on to the story-telling phase.

Projection

From the age of about two years, Piaget maintains that the child becomes aware of the difference between self and others (Miller 1983: 53). This is the stage of preconceptual thought and, according to Erikson, of 'initiation versus guilt' and 'industry versus inadequacy'. It is during this stage that the child experiences a shift to becoming aware of the world outside themselves. Objects and toys take on significance and can therefore be used to tell stories, make up plays, retell the past or explore the future.

In addition to the Thumb Game and the Truth Game (see the supporting exercises and activities at the end of this chapter), I have found projective play with small figures, animals, people, characters and objects most useful in assessing the child. In the initial stages of the relationship, focusing on external objects allows the child to connect with something other than the therapist. Eye contact is not necessarily required, and the child is given time and space to engage with the therapist when he feels ready. With some children even verbal comment is not required. The therapist can merely observe and, if appropriate, make her own comments. Suggestions that the child choose an object to represent himself and members of his family, friends or other significant people in his life may tell a trained therapist much about that child's particular situation and current difficulties.

Depending on the conceptual ability of the child these objects may then be used to make up a story which may give further clues as to the underlying problems. At this stage the child is beginning to use his imagination and through the imagination with the use of projected play he can begin to explore his hopes and fears. He can rehearse and explore the possibilities of the future and attempt to make sense of the past.

For many children their past lives are a jumble of unconnected events, often tragic or violent. By using the figures which represent, albeit subconsciously, the different times and characters in his past, the child can begin to put these in some sort of sequence, or container. I have found that many children enjoy using miniature fences to surround their undesirable characters. Jessica, whose abusive grandfather had exerted an unhealthy control over the family, spent a long time putting all the farm animals into a pen and then allowing them to escape one by one while the bad farmer wasn't looking. She then locked the same farmer up in his own pen.

Similarly, Scott, who had a history of moving from place to place sometimes with and sometimes without his mother, took a great deal of enjoyment from creating little scenes in the Rainbow Room from small figures and material to represent the different places he had lived and the different characters involved. He then spent much time sitting in each of these places and playing with the figures, remembering the good times and the bad. For each place we made sure that there was something good to be remembered there. Being able to explore, acknowledge and then compartmentalise the past while being witnessed is an important process for many children whether the whole story remains in the land of metaphor as with Jessica or is rooted in reality as with Scott. The value of remaining within the metaphor is discussed in Chapter 3 and the power of witnessing in Chapter 4.

Toys may also be used as transitional objects in attachment issues. Bowlby (1969) puts forward the theory that problems may occur in later stages of development for a child for whom there has been early separation from the mother, and Winnicott (1971) expounds the idea that a toy or something that smells of or belongs to the primary carer may be of help over the separation period. Sarah, whose dream 'The Stone of Life' emphasised the anxiety she was feeling about her impending adolescence and separation from her mother, found that a semi-precious stone that her mother had bought her which symbolised protection was of help in being able to sleep.

Puppets fall into a category between projective play and role play and can be a very useful medium for a child who needs to speak through the object but is not yet able or willing to take on a role. Andrew, through his story 'The Alien Mr Giraffe' explored his lack of social awareness through close identification with and speaking through the Mr Clown puppet. The part of Andrew that understood appropriate social communication was given licence to speak through the Mr Clown puppet. The depth of identification needed to achieve this result would not have been readily available through a projective object and was inaccessible to Andrew through role.

Role

As a child progresses through projective play they will, as a norm, gradually begin to introduce more dramatic qualities into their play. They are more inclined to want to speak as the character and the character may begin to have adventures of its own. As an initial exercise in role I will often invite the child to dress up as his favourite character from a book, play or film. William's self-confidence was greatly increased by taking on the role of Batman, and, although he was unable to continue to use the medium of role play to explore his ongoing difficult feelings, it was from this newly empowered position that he gave me his story 'The Magic Book'.

It is from the age of about seven years onwards that a child is able to make use of role play. According to Piaget this is the age when one begins to have the ability to take on others' points of view and to see oneself as others. Erikson sees this stage as 'identity versus role' confusion (Miller 1983: 169) and this theory underpins much of the work done by Landy (1993) with regards to the importance of having one's own repertoire of functional roles. The significance of extending one's repertoire through role play is discussed in Chapter 4.

Once a child has progressed to being able to use the medium of role there are many techniques which may be used to help them explore the reasons for their behaviour or their hidden emotions and motives. One of these is a technique called Role Reversal which, used successfully by a trained therapist, can result in a child seeing a different viewpoint, achieving an understanding or accessing an unrecognised skill or knowledge. Andrew, by 'becoming' the socially aware Mr Clown in his story of 'The Alien Mr Giraffe' was shocked by Mr Giraffe's behaviour into accessing his own unrecognised standards of appropriate behaviour. Similarly, Sophie and Amber, by playing through scenarios in which they took on the roles of the abusive or neglectful adult, achieved an understanding of how this form of behaviour did not achieve positive outcomes and was therefore not to be copied; a decision which was manifested in their story 'The Queen Who Shouted'.

Another technique, which I have found especially useful in working with children's dreams, is that of a version of the Empty Chair, a procedure which has been adopted from psychodrama. It involves the child speaking as if they were the other person or creature in their story. Using this technique Jenny was able to speak as the man who had frightened her in her story 'The Scary Man', discover that he meant her no harm and reframe the ending of her dream so that it no longer haunted or worried her. In the same way, by dialoguing with the alien creatures in her story 'The Nasty Aliens', Christie was able to discover what they represented and, with help, change the situation. In these scenarios it is important to let the child have the last word speaking as themselves since therein lies the empowerment.

Dramatic play is crucial to a child's development. Through dramatic play a child can reduce the world to a size where it is manageable and where the events of everyday reality can be played out in comparative safety. Jennings (1995: 98) states that 'The dramatic imagination is crucial for survival, as without it we would not be able to imagine how things might be or how they could be, or indeed we would not be able to hypothesize.'

Normal progression through these three stages of embodiment–projection–role is that which is to be hoped for in the healthy development of a child. Jennings (1995: 97) says that the 'passage through these three stages...contribute to the emergence of character.' It is when this development has been arrested due to negative influences that the opportunity offered by dramatherapy to revisit and rework the particular stage in a positive way is so valuable.

Supporting exercises and activities

Assessment

In addition to the assessment techniques described in this chapter that would require training as a therapist, the following are exercises which I have found useful in determining the difficulties currently facing a child:

The thumb game

- Explain to the child (depending on age) that you have a 'magic' thumb.
- Explain that when it is pointing downwards it means the child is completely sad, and when it is pointing upwards the child is really happy.
- Start at the bottom and invite the child to say 'Stop' when he feels that is where he is.
- This game is very useful for a quick, non-verbal check on how the child is feeling and, in my experience, is surprisingly accurate.

The truth game

- Explain to the child that you are going to make some guesses as to what is wrong. Care should be taken to make these guesses non-specific, for example, 'Something is wrong at school?'
- Explain that if you are right they can take a step towards you and if you are wrong they can take a step away.
- Keep the game very light-hearted and general.
- If they reach you, the chances are that they will want to tell you more.
- If they reach the door, the situation is probably better left and approached in another way.

Summary

Embodiment–projection–role – a process employed by the Creative Expressive model of dramatherapy is a useful way of working with children in school.

- The embodiment–projection–role process corresponds generally to the developmental theories of Piaget and Erikson.

- Problems may arise when these stages are not progressed through normally and dramatherapy can be helpful here as a means of revisiting these stages.

- The embodiment stage, corresponding to when a child first becomes aware of self, encourages the child to express himself through his senses.

- The embodiment stage is useful as an introduction to emotional literacy and as a grounding and anchoring exercise.

- The projection stage occurs from the age of about two years onwards when a child becomes aware of self and others; encourage the child to project himself through the use of other objects, small figures, toys etc.

- The projection stage has been found to be the most useful in terms of assessment for primary school children.

- The role stage is accessible from about the age of seven onwards when a child is able to see himself as others.

- The role stage lends itself to many and varied dramatic techniques which can be exploited for therapeutic outcomes.

- Through dramatic play a child can rehearse the confusing and unmanageable events of everyday reality.

Chapter 3
The Significance of Metaphor and Symbol in Dramatherapy

You see it's like a portmanteau – there are two meanings packed up into one word. (Alice Through The Looking Glass, Lewis Carroll)

Metaphor and symbol: a definition

A dictionary definition explains the word 'metaphor' as being a figure of speech in which a word or phrase is applied to an object or action that it does not literally denote in order to apply a resemblance, and the word 'symbol' as something that represents or stands for something else, usually by convention or association. Both definitions refer to the fact that the language of metaphor and symbolism is an alternative way of expression, a way which, as we will see, is more conducive to a child's emotional needs than the conventional language-based means of explanation.

Jungian concepts

Much dramatherapeutic work centres on the ideas of the psychologist Carl Gustav Jung (1875–1961) who, having been a pupil of Sigmund Freud, diverted from Freud's way of thinking in 1913 to devise his own system of psychoanalysis. One of Jung's major contentions was that life has meaning and that this meaning can be understood and experienced symbolically. Jung believed that the inner world of the unconscious communicated with our ego self through a language of spontaneous images and symbols and that these images and symbols had a compensatory function counterbalancing deficiencies or one-sided tendencies of the conscious ego standpoint. It was this principle which underpinned the intervention in the case of Natalie and her stories of 'The Crowded House' and 'The Kidnapping' in that it was a belief that the 'voices' had something of value to impart that led to the subsequent method of treatment. It is also this belief which is behind much of the dream work which I have done with children, as for example, with Christie and her dream 'The Nasty Aliens'.

Jung further maintained that this leaning towards compensation implied a 'Wholeness' towards which the psyche was naturally inclined. The unconscious is constantly informing us, through dreams, daydreams and spontaneous thought and actions, of ways in which we may strive towards 'Wholeness'. Dramatherapy is a way of helping to interpret the unconscious and with children, for whom spontaneous thought and action is natural, it is a natural and obvious way to encourage them towards achieving this mental stability.

Through dramatherapy the images and symbols of the unconscious mind can be consciously engaged with – for example through the re-enactment of dreams. When this happens, the energy contained in the symbols is transformed which allows a new stage of psychic development to begin.

Jungian ways of working

The Creative Expressive model of dramatherapy is very largely based on Jungian ways of working. Creative Projection uses sand play, clay work and body movement in order to express fantasy material. Active Imagination techniques work with fantasy in the awake state, for example through story telling or dream re-enactment.

Metaphor: the link between left and right brain

In creative problem-solving, two phases corresponding to the two modes of the brain are necessary. The solution or 'healing' needs not only to be thought out by the logical, reasoning, analytical left brain which orders speech and language, but also 'felt' by the creative, perceptive right brain responsible for parallel processing and spatial/depth perception. This could explain why dramatherapy is so often effective in that it is '. . . a procedure that moves from talking to creative action where the client is encouraged to let go, play in space, integrate action, imagination, feeling, thought' (Casson 1998: 13).

Metaphor can be used to facilitate this procedure. Metaphor, from the Greek origin meaning to 'carry across', transfers images which may be emotionally based from the right to the left brain where they can be given meaning through language. According to Casson metaphor makes the transition from inner to outer reality where fantasy can be expressed and translated into everyday meaning. 'Metaphor' he says, 'is a bridge between worlds' (Casson 1998: 14).

Usefulness to the therapist

The notion of metaphor is central to dramatherapy in that it allows the therapist to gather information indirectly. As much of the information which is forthcoming in dramatherapy sessions does not emanate directly from the logical, analytical left brain, it is therefore not thought out or intellectual but rather personal, direct and spontaneous. It might be said that it comes more 'from the heart'. It has consequently not been through the left-brain process of analysis and judgement where much of what is nevertheless true might be filtered out for appearances' sake. Metaphor is a means of conveying this 'truth'.

Metaphor and symbol are also useful to the dramatherapist in that they help to preserve confidentiality. Very often, and especially with younger children, the whole therapeutic intervention will remain within the land of story and no allusion will ever be made as to the reality from which the fantasy material springs. As all remains within the realm of the symbolic, the child may begin to accept the meaning as or when he is ready – peeling off the layers of fantasy which cover the core of truth rather like peeling off the layers of an onion. As has been said above, he may never make that final connection with the link to his everyday reality and all may remain within his unconscious to surface at a much later date. Bettelheim (1991: 279), in his work on the symbolism and metaphor in fairy tales, said that:

Since all is expressed in symbolic language . . . the child can disregard what he is not ready for by responding only to what he has been told on the surface. But he is also enabled to peel off, layer by layer, some of the meaning hidden behind the symbol as he becomes gradually ready and able to master and profit from it.

The clinical psychologist Birgitte Brun maintains that symbols are linked with various drives and may have a 'regulating impact on our actions like a stop and go mechanism' (Brun *et al.* 1993: 7). Young as they are, many children have built up huge defence mechanisms against emotional experiences which may inhibit their potential to learn and change. If symbols with their direct link to the unconscious are used, the repressed emotions are freed, which in turn 'increases the potential to learn, sets associations free and adds colour and strength to our experience of living' (Brun *et al.* 1993: 8).

Thus, by staying within the land of story – of metaphor and symbolism – the process has a twofold benefit. It can be taken at the pace of the child, and by remaining within the 'unknowing' the confidentiality of the child's story may be preserved. This is especially important in a group situation. Stacey's monster in her story 'The Red and Orange Monster' was never analysed, there was no need and it would have betrayed an important confidentiality to do so. Stacey's 'healing' took place nevertheless. How much she understood of the symbolic nature of tackling the monster on her own will remain with her.

Furthermore, and most importantly, direct interpretation of the symbolic and metaphoric language used by a child is difficult if not downright dangerous for we all have our own personal and very different dictionary of symbols. It is for this reason that no explanation is offered of the stories included in this book, and an understanding of the way in which the story has helped the child is left to the judgement of the reader.

Usefulness to child

As has already been explained, metaphor and symbol are the language of the unconscious, and their importance to the world of children is incalculable. According to Piaget (1970), in early childhood cognitive abilities with regard to the abstract are not yet developed. This makes the processing of abstract thoughts and concepts very difficult. Bettelheim says that 'the child's unconscious processes can only become clarified for him through images which speak to the unconscious' (1991: 31).

With children who have suffered from abuse or neglect these psychological processes may also provide a mechanism for safety and may be used by much older children. In her story 'Through The Wall' Diana was able to confront her past through the medium of a tale about 'another child' and only when her conscious mind was ready did it acknowledge the connection between the main character Sara's story and her own.

Bettelheim, having spent much time in concentration camps and studying the links between behaviour and pressures of the unconscious, put forward the argument that story is a very useful medium in that it can act as a filter preventing unconscious-damaging material from entering the conscious mind directly where it could be dangerous (Bettelheim 1991). The pain that the conscious mind is thus allowed to feel is only relative to its coping ability. Dramatherapy is a way of holding and staying with this emotional pain. Douglas, in his story 'The Pointed Diamond', allowed himself to experience the pain that his death would cause his mother, experimenting with a degree of emotion which was not forthcoming in real life.

And thus it was that Lori in her story 'The Two Princesses and the Walled Castle', through symbolising the abusive adult in the form of 'the bad man', was able to stay with and explore her past and present fear and emotional pain, finally making a positive and successful attempt to overcome them.

How does it work?

As has already been stated, dramatherapy deals with unacknowledged and confused feelings. Metaphor gives expression to these feelings by its very nature and power. A child's mind works in images and it might be said that images are metaphors for feelings. Therefore we might say that the feelings of a child are expressed through images which are carried over by means of metaphor to a space made available by dramatherapy where they may be dealt with in whichever way the child's psyche deems appropriate.

In my work as a dramatherapist I do not deal with the feelings. I maintain that my work is not to 'sort things out' for the child but to provide the necessary conditions for the child to 'sort things out' for themselves. Like Mann (1996: 4) I would argue that, 'Dramatherapists have a primary task of setting the scene for healing rather than actually contriving to heal.'

It is this fundamental belief in the power of the mind to heal itself given the right conditions which underpins much of my work. To look at the child in the light of what in him is healthy and sound rather than in terms of his defects is not only another Jungian concept but also a guiding principle in dramatherapy. To believe that the mind's inherent inclination towards 'Wholeness' is capable of overcoming any tendencies to unhealthy deviations, given the right conditions, is to empower both therapist and child.

Summary

- The language of metaphor and symbol is an alternative way of expression conducive to a child's emotional needs.

- Dramatherapy adopts the ideas of Jung in believing that the unconscious mind communicates through a language of images and symbol.

- Dramatherapy methods of creative expression are a means of 'downloading' what our unconscious wishes us to know at a pace that it wishes us to know it.

- Metaphor is crucial to creative problem-solving for a child in that it 'carries over' emotionally charged images from the right brain to the left where they can be put into language.

- Metaphor is a means of conveying these emotional truths as they emanate from the non-judgemental right brain.

- Confidentiality and emotional and psychological safety for the child may be preserved by allowing the therapeutic intervention to remain within the realms of metaphor and symbol.

- Direct interpretation of metaphor and symbol is not advised.

- Cognitive abstract abilities in the very young child are usually undeveloped hence an unspoken language is often needed to express their feelings.

- These feelings can be expressed in images carried over by metaphor and explored via dramatherapy.

- The contention is that the dramatherapist is responsible for setting the scene, not for providing the healing.

- Dramatherapy can provide the vehicle for the holding of emotional pain.

- The dramatherapeutic methods used here focus on what is healthy and sound in the child and on the power of the child's mind to heal itself.

Chapter 4

The Value of Personal Story Telling

Johnnie, the peppermint pig, gone now like this whole long year of her life, but fixed and safe in her mind, for ever and ever. (The Peppermint Pig, Nina Bawden)

What is Personal Story Telling?

For me, Personal Story Telling is an attempt to make sense of one's life, to relate and have witnessed the events and experiences of life so that they may be added up and some sort of meaning derived from them. Whitmont (1991: ix) says that 'To be an actor in one's life drama without understanding its dramatic thrust...makes it meaningless at best and chaotic at worst...What has meaning can be better borne...Chaotic suffering is unbearable.'

Thus, it is that by providing a safe space and a certain quality of attention a dramatherapist may be able to facilitate the arrival of a child at some point of acceptance and understanding of their lives. Very often this will not be at a conscious level but will remain, as has already been discussed, within the realms of metaphor and symbol. The jumble of events that only too often seem to pack a child's life seem insurmountable when viewed en masse. By taking each event, untangling it from the jumble, viewing it in its entirety and then putting it in sequence, the insurmountable mass may become compartmentalised and therefore more easily assimilated as it was with Scott in Chapter 2.

The dramatherapeutic space and Personal Story Telling technique also give the child the freedom to externalise and explore the feelings which may evolve from real-life events. Peter Slade, well known for his work on child drama explained how, to manage the unhappy feelings his experiences at boarding school gave him, he and his friends used to 'move off to the downs and do violent athletic dance and improvised drama about the hated masters. We killed them all off. We always returned to school refreshed' (cited in Langley 1995/6: 2). By replaying events which hold emotional tension within a safely structured framework the child can also regain some of the control which he has lost in real life. In real life the masters had control over and mastery of Slade; empowerment came for him when, through drama, he turned the tables. Lori, in her story 'The Two Princesses and the Walled Castle', felt this sense of empowerment when she gained control over 'the bad man' even going so far as to overcome her own boundaries and venture outside the castle walls to make sure he was dead.

The element of being in control and having the ability to make choices is an important benefit derived from Personal Story Telling. It often occurs naturally in non-directive play when the child is free to 'make up' his own story. Given the liberty to do so, the child will normally cast himself in a more empowered role with greater freedom of choice than is the fact in everyday reality. There are occasions when the child chooses to play the victim, and then work on his functional role repertoire may be required (see this chapter's section on the meaning and value of role playing, p. 17). There are also various techniques which may be used to direct the story telling towards the inclusion of making choices as with the six-part storyboard which will be explained later in this chapter.

Ritual and times of change

Childhood is a time of many changes, one of the most significant being the onset of puberty. It is a time when hormones run riot and emotions with them. And yet little or no attention is paid to this enormously significant occurrence in mainstream education. In traditional societies rituals took place during times of change guiding and helping the individual through the difficult period; in the case of puberty, rituals allowing the youngster to establish his own social identity and confirming his role as an adult. Nowadays we have no such rituals. Renée Emunah, founder/director of the dramatherapy programme at the California Institute of Integral Studies, who has worked with emotionally disturbed youngsters for more than 16 years says that 'the lack of community, of extended family, of meaningful avenues for expression or ways of demonstrating worthiness and of ritual all contribute to adolescent alienation' (Emunah 1995: 153).

Providing the opportunity to explore a time of transition by using ritual in the dramatherapeutic space may allow a child to look ahead to the future while assimilating the past. Sarah, after her dream 'The Stone of Life', was given this opportunity by playing through the symbolic ritual of transferring from the baby island to the grown-up island. She was given the chance to decide which island she preferred and whether or not she wanted to make the change. It was Sarah and not I who made the choice and Sarah and not I who threw away the stepping stones thus making the decision irreversible and confirming it in her psyche.

The changes which take place during childhood may not always be internal. For any child a change of one of the following: house, parent or carer, school, friends and immediate or extended family grouping can have a substantial effect. Many children who come to me have experienced not just one but many changes in, again, not just one but all of the above. The child who experiences these changes is required to be adaptable in the extreme. The obvious scenario is that they learn not to care too deeply, for whatever they care about may be taken away from them with the next breath.

Alida Gersie, a Senior Lecturer in Post-Graduate Arts Therapies and well known for her work in story telling explains that 'Stories are often told in times of transition' (Gersie 1992: 33). They can provide reassurance which then helps to strengthen the motivation to change. By retelling events that have happened in his own life, whether as fact or through metaphor, the child can distance himself from them as he would if they were part of a real story. By distancing himself he is then more able to view the events from an objective viewpoint and the inherent changes may seem less devastating, less overwhelming.

The role of the witness

An important contributor to the power of a ritual is the witness. By being held in positive, non-judgemental regard the child is emboldened to be himself and display his hopes and fears. These hopes and fears are then accepted by the witness, in this case the dramatherapist and, by their very acceptance, are given value. A child suffering from very low self-esteem will often feel that he and, thus, his hopes and fears are not important enough to be given any time and consideration; a message that may frequently have been passed down to him from adults. By accepting, considering and giving time to the child, the dramatherapist may be able to reflect his emotions back to him thus helping to contain his fears and validate his hopes.

For many children the events of their lives and the emotions which they give rise to are too shocking to be admitted. By becoming the unshockable witness the dramatherapist can encourage the uncovering of these events and emotions from the shadowy depths where they have been hidden and where they will nearly always be a source of discomfort at a later date. Misunderstandings arising from a child's over-fertile imagination – for example, the very common misconception that they are somehow to blame for their parents' separation – can also be ironed out.

The meaning and value of role play

The telling of a child's own story can take place in various ways and through various means. A child who is not ready for or not happy with role play will often prefer to use the small figures and tell their story through projected play (see Chapter 2 on embodiment–projection–role). The ability to put oneself in another's shoes, to see as another sees and therefore to take on a role is a developmental stage normally not reached until about the age of seven. This, of course, is a very general statement and is not true of some children who may be much older than seven but who may not have progressed beyond the stage of projective play because for some reason, usually abuse, neglect or trauma, their development has been arrested. Similarly I have met very young children who display an astonishing ability to empathise and see themselves as others, which belies their background and their age.

On the whole, how engaged a child is with playing out the role of a character within their story reflects the extent to which the character is a part of themselves. We each have our own system of roles which we parade at different times depending on the circumstances. These roles may be functional or dysfunctional. Through dramatherapy, different roles may be called forth, explored and either substantiated or discarded. The aim is to create a functional and viable role system where the positive and negative qualities that exist in all of us may be tolerated; to discover new ways of reacting to others which are more useful and then, through role play, to rehearse these roles in a rehearsal-for-life scenario. Radmall (1995: 22) maintains that it is through the taking on of different roles that one can extend one's role system so that 'one is no longer required to behave in a certain way' and is free from the 'unspoken assumptions [which] may be internalised and [...may] influence and restrict'.

These roles or subpersonalities, as they are often called, exist to protect our core. Thus we may play the role of victim or bully to protect the vulnerable self. As a rule, those subpersonalities of which we are not aware, which have been pushed back into the subconscious, into the 'Shadow', as Jung would term it, are often those which cause problems. The child who constantly plays the victim may not be aware that there is a bully inside him. Through dramatherapy and the spontaneous, creative right-brained approach, the child may access this previously unrecognised role of the bully, explore it in an atmosphere of acceptance and safety and take from the role those aspects he would like to keep, such as strength, courage, standing up for oneself, while rejecting those qualities which are not useful such as manipulation and cruelty.

The importance of de-roling

After any period of enactment when the child has taken on another role it is extremely important that the process of de-roling or 'taking off the character' be undertaken. This is to ensure that the child does not return to the classroom still believing, for example, that he is a monster or a baby when inappropriate and unfortunate behaviour might ensue. Depending on the engagement of the child with the character in question this process may take five seconds or five minutes. A suggested procedure is to ask the child to take off the character as if he were taking off an imaginary cloak and say something along the lines of 'I am not _____, I am (and state their own name)'. In a group session this can be done in turn with the group witnessing, and can be quite powerful. If this procedure is not adequate then the child may be asked to sit on one chair and speak as the character and then on another chair and speak as himself. With older children this process can include speaking as the character and reflecting on their thoughts and actions and then speaking as themselves and reflecting on the character's thoughts and actions as if they were a third person. The extent to which a child is able to do this is an assessment of their ability to objectify and distance themselves from their emotions – an important step in gaining emotional literacy.

The objective therefore is to encourage the child to be aware of all the roles he plays so that he may build up a complete system of functional roles which he may use in his everyday life. The value for the child of telling his own story is not only to bring to light the different roles he plays, but also for him to be able to play out the roles of other characters in his story thus enabling him to see situations from an objective and non-ego-centred point of view. By acknowledging and reflecting on the feelings of the character in his story the child is building up his own storehouse of emotional literacy. To what extent a child is able to distance himself from and comment upon the character he has just played afterwards is an indication of how far he has come along the road of personal awareness and emotional stability.

Sometimes a character in a child's story will resemble that of an archetype when the traits observed are no longer purely personal but seem instead to belong to the collection of universal human patterns. Archetypes will be further discussed in Chapter 5, use of pre-written material.

The main purpose of Personal Story Telling is, therefore, empowerment for the child through self-awareness. Central to this issue of empowerment is the element of choice. In everyday reality the child may feel he has no choice and therefore no control. Very often he has been catapulted into a 'fight or flight' reaction. By replaying and consequently slowing down the series of events the child is given time to acknowledge, consider and plan out his course of action or reaction. He is given a choice and therefore control. With choice and control his self-esteem and self-confidence rises.

The six-part story method

The six-part story method was developed to try to identify coping strategies in individuals at the Community Stress Prevention Centre in northern Israel, which works with both the Arab and Israeli communities. Because of the high levels of military, paramilitary and terrorist activity which have existed in the area for over 30 years there is a high level of stress in the surrounding communities. The six-part story method was introduced as an attempt to let the creative, illogical right brain have its say in an assessment which had hitherto only used techniques to reach the left brain. Both Mooli Lahad, who was the originator of the six-part story method and Alida Gersie, another expert in this story-telling technique, use 'story making as a therapeutic technique for clients to project their own stories based on elements contained in fairytales or myths' (Jennings *et al.* 1994: 24).

In my own work I have found an adaptation of the above method to be very useful both as an aid to diagnosis and assessment and as a structure which guides the child to tell his own story through metaphor. This is particularly useful when there is a need to establish a distancing from the real-life material and the child is unable to come up with his own metaphorical language of explanation (see Chapter 3 on the significance of metaphor and symbol). The formula of 'hero/heroine, mission, helpmate, obstacles or monster, coping strategies or means of overcoming – and ending' (see below) is one which gives the child a framework within which to explore his secret desires (through the hero and the mission), the difficulties in his life (through the monster) and his way of coping or overcoming these difficulties by arriving at a satisfactory conclusion.

The element of choice is also inherent in this method – for example, in the choice of the helpmate – and may constitute the most important part of the process in that it represents the way in which the child chooses to help himself and to bring about his own healing. In some cases, as with Stacey in her story of 'The Red and Orange Monster' it may be that the child elects to overcome the obstacle without the helpmate as the helpmate has threatened to take over.

I have found the six-part story method to be a valuable technique in encouraging children to tell their own stories in that it is a safe and structured framework which provides the children with opportunities to make decisions and choices and to exercise their own free will and control within clear boundaries. In doing so the child's sense of empowerment, self-esteem and self-confidence is greatly increased.

In addition, the child's awareness of, and control over, the roles he plays may be enhanced by being able to comment afterwards on the characters in the storyboard, their choice of a helpmate and their methods of dealing with the difficulties in their lives.

Personal Story Telling through dramatherapy is, therefore, a method by which children can express themselves in their own language but within a safe and structured framework and receive the rewards of being acknowledged and accepted for doing so.

Supporting exercises and activities

The six-part story method

Although it is not recommended that this method be used for assessment or diagnostic purposes unless by a trained professional, it can safely be used in the following format to help a child towards self-expression and feelings of empowerment through choice. It is particularly useful with children suffering from low self-esteem or self-confidence. It is important to allow whatever story the child tells to remain within the land of story. Unless specific training has been received it is advised that the adult merely accepts the child's story with minimum comment.

- Using an A4 sheet of paper and a pencil divide the paper into six squares to resemble a cartoon storyboard.
- Tell the child to write the following titles in the squares (or, depending on the age and maturity of the child, write them yourself):
    Square 1: the hero or heroine
    Square 2: the mission
    Square 3: the helpmate
    Square 4: the obstacles or monster they will meet
    Square 5: how they overcome these
    Square 6: the ending.
- Ask the child to draw pictures under the headings. They may wish to make it a cartoon and use speech or thought bubbles.

- Help the child to think of a satisfactory ending where the monster/difficulty is overcome.
- If appropriate, act out the above story in a group making sure that the child whose story it is plays the role of the hero or heroine. You may wish to explain that everyone will have a turn and that it is always the child whose story it is who is the 'director' and who directs how the story will unfold.
- De-role by asking the children, one by one, to mime taking off the character they have just been playing as if it were an article of clothing and saying 'I am not _____, I am (their name)'.

Summary

- Personal Story Telling is an attempt to relate and have witnessed the events and experiences of a child's life through the medium of story so that they may be better understood and accepted.

- Personal Story Telling also allows the child to be in control and to make choices in situations which are normally out of his control.

- Personal Story Telling gives the child the freedom to externalise and explore feelings which may evolve from real-life events.

- Rituals, through the medium of story telling, can be helpful in times of change and transition.

- The role of the unshockable, accepting, non-judgemental witness is paramount in containing the fears of the child and substantiating his hopes and dreams.

- The playing out of different characters in Personal Story Telling allows the child to explore a repertoire of more functional roles which he may use in real life thus raising his self-awareness.

- The main purpose of Personal Story Telling is empowerment through self-awareness and increased emotional literacy.

- The six-part story method is a useful technique for introducing a structure into Personal Story Telling where one may be needed.

- The act of de-roling should always be undertaken after any enactment.

- Personal Story Telling allows a child to express himself in his own way through his own language within a safe, structured framework and to be accepted and rewarded for doing so.

The Stories

THE WATER PRINCESS

Angela   Age 11y

Bereavement

Eight weekly sessions

The background

Angela was a shy, sensitive child of 11 whose mother had died of a particularly virulent form of cancer. At first Angela seemed to be managing well with the support that she received from her family and the school. Her younger brother had had temper tantrums at school and at home and Angela had helped her father deal with these. Her younger sister had appeared to revert to baby-ish behaviour for a while, but then had turned to the grandmother as a mother substitute. Angela had shown very few signs of grief and had been a great support to her father in the home. After some months the school noticed that Angela's work was beginning to deteriorate. A bright child, she no longer showed enthusiasm for anything, frequently bursting into tears and seeming reluctant to mix with her friends, preferring the company of one or two sympathetic female teachers. Then she began to have the odd day's absence; on querying this the school learnt that her father was having a great deal of trouble in persuading Angela to come to school at all. Angela was becoming a school refuser.

Angela was shy at working on a one-to-one basis at first, but she soon realised that nothing was expected of her and that she was free to do, or not do, whatever she wished. After some sessions of trust-building games and exercises and some projection work using the small figures she was ready to move on to making up and acting out her own stories. On this particular occasion she used blue and green material to transform the small Rainbow Room into an ocean. The following is her story.

Once upon a time there lived a water princess. She lived in a big ocean and swam all day long in the waves. She talked to all the fish who lived there and they were all her friends. When they were sick she looked after them and she made them better. Everyone loved her. She didn't have a family because she didn't need a family with all the fish as friends. She was friendly with the mermaids too and used to borrow their combs to comb her hair. It wasn't long and golden like theirs but brown and wavy. When it rained she used to come out of the sea and sit on a rock and then dance in the sand because she loved the rain. If the sun shone as well and there was a rainbow she climbed up one side and slid down the other. Nobody knew how old she was for it seemed as if she had been there forever. One summer it didn't rain for a very long time and all the fishes and little sea crea-tures were very worried because the water princess had disappeared. They all kept asking each other if anyone had seen her but nobody had. The crabs looked under the sand and the eels looked in the craggy rocks. The baby seahorses went off in great families to look for her but no one could find her. One day a party of sea creatures went down to visit the old wise man who lived at the bottom of the sea. He told them not to worry and that the water princess would be back – when it rained; that she was always there but that they just couldn't see her. And sure enough one night it rained. There was a big storm and the raindrops fell like big stones into the sea. In the morning the water princess was there sitting on her favourite rock and combing her hair and singing. And the little fishes and sea creatures were never worried again for they knew that even if the water princess seemed to disappear she was never really very far away.

The outcome

Angela was extremely energised after this story. She worked on it over a number of weeks taking the part of the water princess herself and seemed to acquire a self-empowerment through doing so. Angela's mother had loved the sea. One of her last trips before she died had been to her favourite beach. She had told Angela that she would always be with her whenever she was near water, by the sea or in the drops of rain. Although Angela had recognised this cognitively, by taking on the role of the water princess herself, identifying with the character and being witnessed, she was able to acquire a degree of acceptance which led to her being able to move on. Angela slowly started to integrate back into school life. Her odd days off became fewer and her work began to improve. She no longer needed to blot out the pain of losing her mother by trying to take her mother's place in the family. She is currently a noisy teenager with string of GCSEs and a boyfriend and is driving her father mad!

N.B. Supporting exercises and activities to help with loss and bereavement are to be found in Chapter 7, Working with Loss and Bereavement.

THE MAGIC BOOK

William   Age 8y

Place in family, lack of self-esteem

Six weekly sessions and ongoing support

The background

William, aged eight, is the middle child in the family with an older brother and a younger sister. He had been referred by his teacher because of ongoing disruptive behaviour in class. There had been a history of this over the years with no apparent reason. His mother had been very supportive, coming into school to see teachers whenever asked. The father was more elusive and seldom referred to. The older brother had had problems in school, usually to do with anger outbursts, but nothing on the scale of William's behaviour. The younger sister was very pretty and no trouble in the reception class.

Upon asking about William it was learnt that other teachers and classroom assistants had had some anxieties about him over the years. There had been no major problems, but his tendency to close up, to refuse to talk or volunteer any information at all about the reasons for his behaviour had been regarded as odd and somewhat worrying. He had been referred to the Behavioural Support Team with temporarily pleasing results, but his behaviour had deteriorated over the previous few weeks.

On his first visit, through using the little figures, William volunteered the information that he would like to be closer to his elder brother and to 'get rid of' his little sister. Using the six-part storyboard, William's hero Batman did not have his own mission in life but was 'told' a mission by his boss. After the storyboard had been completed, and when asked if Batman had ever had any ideas of his own, William replied 'no, he wouldn't be allowed to and he would be shouted at if he tried.'

William was happy to act out the storyboard as it stood. Afterwards I gave William, as Batman, the opportunity to find his own mission. Batman steadfastly refused and seemed scared to try.

We then moved back from role playing into the comparative safety of projection by using a story game. Without looking, William drew the card with the face of a little boy who looked upset. (It is interesting, more often than not, how uncannily relevant the cues appear!)

On being asked why the little boy was upset and what would make it better, William told the following story.

Once upon a time there was a little boy who had a sister and she had a magic book. This meant that she could have everything she wanted whenever she wanted it. More than anything else in the world the little boy wanted a magic book like hers.

So one day he decided to do something about it. While she was out he crept upstairs and grabbed the book. He knew he couldn't keep it so he just looked on the inside cover to see where it had come from.

It said

The Wizard in the Woods

France

So one night when the house was sleeping the little boy crept out and made his way to the Wizard's house. He knocked on the door and asked the Wizard for a book just like his sister's.

The Wizard said that he could have one – an even better one – but that he would have to use it wisely and share it because magic had to be used wisely. If he didn't use it wisely and share the book he would have to give it back.

The little boy said that he would remember this but when he got home found that, try as he might, he couldn't bring himself to share the book. All he wanted to say to his sister was 'I've got a better book than you'.

One day when he went to pick up the book he opened it at the page which showed the Wizard's face. The face spoke to him and it said, 'You have forgotten your promise little boy. The book must be returned.'

So the little boy took the book back to the Wizard's house and very sadly gave it back to him. 'Thank you for bringing back the book,' the Wizard said. 'Remember that it is here and that it is yours to claim whenever you want to – whenever you think you can use it wisely and share it with others.'

The little boy went home. He was sad, but he knew that one day he would return and claim his book.

The outcome

Behaviour is a form of social conduct and communication. William, through his behaviour was trying to communicate something. That 'something' was not being heard. Only once you have been heard and understood can you move on. Through dramatherapy William was managing to communicate and be heard.

This story involved a learning curve for both William and I. The search for the magic book which would empower the little boy and give him the same ability to please and be accepted as his sister, felt as if it was of enormous significance to William. It was therefore with a sense of deep disappointment that I received the ending of the story in which the little boy was unable to reach a level of emotional maturity which could accommodate his new-found powers of self-esteem. In this William was the wiser, the realist, and I learnt the necessity of resisting the impulse to 'make it all right' and have a happy ending.

William is still working with me. Batman has begun to have a few ideas of his own without either William or I openly acknowledging the fact. The classroom and playtime behaviour has settled somewhat. William is inclined to smile a little more and will now look me in the eyes. One day we will replay the story of the magic book, and one day we will fetch the book home – but it will be in William's time, not mine.

Supporting exercises and activities

Severe loss of self-esteem should always be referred. The following, however, are some ideas which may be helpful in dealing with less acute cases.

Identifying with one's hero or heroine

This technique can be very empowering for children.

- Ask a child for their favourite film/story/fairy-tale character.
- Allow the child to dress up (if possible and appropriate) and play out what this character would do. Follow the child's lead. Never suggest ideas of your own. Anything they say or do will have significance for them and may be thwarted by another intervention.
- Afterwards, praise the good/empowering qualities of the character.
- Ask the child how they think they are like the character and, if appropriate, point out the positive connections between the character's behaviour and that of the child, for example, helpfulness and bravery.
- Depending on the age of the child, ask which positive qualities of their character they would like to keep and which they would like to get rid of. This can be done dramatically by putting on (as a cloak) the good qualities or hugging them to you and throwing away (in an imaginary bin or fire) those qualities not wanted.

The technique is similar to that used in the process of de-roling as discussed in Chapter 4.

The session should always end on a positive note so that the child will go away feeling 'good' and as if they have been listened to.

THE CHILDREN'S ISLAND; FUZZ THE BEAR; THE DANCING BUTTERFLY

Alexa   Age 7y

Neglect and violence in the home

Weekly sessions over 15 months

The background

Alexa was first referred when she was aged seven and she continued to have weekly sessions with me until just before her ninth birthday. She was referred because of concerns about her inability to control her anger and her general disruptive and volatile behaviour in class. She came from a background of neglect and violence; the father was in and out of prison for grievous bodily harm and the mother, having struggled to keep the family together, finally gave up and resorted to drinking heavily. It was frequently Alexa's role to go to the shop to buy something to feed her younger brothers and sisters for breakfast.

In spite of this, Alexa was an optimistic, vivacious child who possessed a lively imagination and a very strong personality. Unfortunately, she was also very sensitive and was constantly in trouble for fighting back over some imagined insult. There was no doubt that she was a survivor but her method of survival was landing her in a lot of trouble both in and out of school. The fear was that unless Alexa learnt to control her emotions a little more she would find herself in serious trouble once she left the more understanding and nurturing confines of the primary school.

From the very first session it was obvious that Alexa felt at home with working with dramatherapy. As soon as a feeling of trust and safety had been established, she allowed her imagination to run free and made maximum use of the sessions by simultaneously making up and acting out stories which sometimes had a cohesive theme and sometimes did not.

A few weeks into the sessions, Alexa came to school one Monday morning in a very bad mood and proceeded to be as disruptive as possible over the next few days. It appeared that her father, recently out of prison and now living elsewhere, had promised that she could visit him over half-term and Alexa had been looking forward to it. It now transpired that this wasn't possible and her mother was going away instead.

Alexa told me how she felt about this. We drew out the feelings by asking Alexa to lie on a long piece of wallpaper and drawing a line around her twice, first to colour in the bad feelings and then a second time to put in the good (see p. 31). We got rid of the bad feelings by tearing them up and we kept the good feelings. We then made an 'anger mountain' out of material (mostly red chosen by Alexa) and Alexa repeatedly burst out from underneath flinging the material everywhere.

When she tired of this she asked if she could make up a story. It went like this.

Once upon a time there was an island. It was very far away and you couldn't get to it very easily. Boats and planes didn't come to it and you had to have permission to go to it anyway. It was owned by one little girl. She was the only one in control of the island. It was very beautiful and had lots of sand and blue sea with mermaids and dolphins in it.

There was something very different about this island though. No grown-ups at all were allowed onto it, only children. The controller of the island looked after all sorts of children there. One day someone came across to the island in a boat and said that they had an abandoned baby and would

the controller look after it? The controller said she would and from then on she had lots of abandoned babies to look after.

Another day someone else came over and said that they had some children who had no parents and would the controller look after them too? The controller said she would and so there were lots of children on her island.

One day some grown-up invaders tried to get to her island, but all the children spotted them and threw coconut shells at them. Then they took them prisoner. But the controller was a kind person and she said that they could go free, but that they must never come back to the island again. So they didn't.

And the controller and the children lived happily ever after on their island.

The outcome

This was one of the many stories that Alexa told which were transparently symbolic of the events in her turbulent young life. Following the sessions she was normally calmer and better able to cope. However, on one occasion I made the mistake of underestimating the degree of distress which she felt and of not giving her enough time to prepare herself again for the outside world after the safety of the sessions with distressing results.

The latest development in her background was that there had been a great deal of talk about the whole family going (in Alexa's word 'escaping') to Australia. There was some inference that this was a necessary step. The insecurity that Alexa felt came through in her play and although she was given plenty of time to explore these feelings, the bell for lunchtime rang early and adequate provision for dealing with these feelings was not made. Alexa made her way from the quiet safety of the Rainbow Room to the noisy dinner hall and the change was too much for her. Within seconds she had hit another child and I had learnt a valuable lesson.

It was also becoming apparent that the hourly sessions once a week on a Tuesday were not sufficient to keep Alexa from getting into the sort of trouble which would undo all the positive steps she had made. Although she managed reasonably well on the Wednesday, Thursday and Friday, on the Monday after a weekend at home she was vulnerable again and liable to 'blip' at the slightest provocation.

A transitional object in the form of a bear named 'Fuzz' was brought in. Fuzz had been given to Alexa by a kind-hearted mealtime assistant. Although he wasn't a new toy there was something very endearing about Fuzz with his lopsided grin, and from the first he went everywhere with Alexa. Alexa was encouraged to tell Fuzz all her feelings during the week so that Fuzz (who had a very good memory) could tell me when we met on the Tuesday.

This strategy appeared to work for a while until Alexa came in to school distraught one Monday morning. Over the weekend, following Alexa's apparent misbehaviour, her mother had taken Fuzz away and had given him to a charity shop. The situation was eventually sorted out and Fuzz returned to Alexa, but the incident remained significant in Alexa's mind as the following story shows.

Once upon a time there was a little girl who lived with her Mum, three brothers, four sisters and teddy bear called Fuzz in a very small house. One of the sisters was nearly grown up; she was eighteen, and one of the brothers was too; he was seventeen.

So when the family moved to a lovely small cottage in the country, this brother and sister didn't come which meant that there was more room. The little girl had a room of her own and she felt very grown up.

Her Mum bought her nice clothes and she felt very happy. She forgot Fuzz.

Then, some time later they all moved again to a place over the water. Fuzz was left behind. One day the little girl was out for a walk and she saw a dinghy. Suddenly she remembered Fuzz. She rowed quickly over the water and there was Fuzz, sitting cold and shivering on the sand. She picked him up in her arms and hugged him. Then she went back to her mother and said, 'I went over the water to get Fuzz.'

The outcome

After some weeks of sessions which included story making and emotional literacy activities, Alexa's behaviour gradually began to improve. The incidence of anger outbursts grew fewer which meant that she was beginning to be rewarded for positive behaviour. This, in turn, helped her self-esteem. She began to talk about how she could help her cousin who apparently had 'problems'. It was decided that it would be constructive if Alexa were seen with another child in her class who was unable to show her feelings at all as this might be helpful for Sharon while providing continuing support for Alexa.

The experiment proved very successful and Sharon began to have eye contact and to volunteer information both in class and in the sessions. Although she did not know it Alexa had fulfilled her desire of helping another child through her difficulties. On the last session that the girls had together before the summer holidays Sharon refused to let Alexa take the leading role and demanded that they share it!

It was decided at the beginning of the new term that Alexa's sessions could be scaled down. She was now only having the occasional tantrum and was nearly always able to explain why she was behaving as she was. At home there were ongoing issues around the lack of money and the father not paying child support. On the whole though, Alexa was altogether more pleasant, helpful and calm. On her penultimate session she acted out the following story.

Once upon a time there was a girl called Jennifer. Jennifer loved dancing and she really wanted to go to dancing lessons. Her Mum always said that she couldn't go because they couldn't afford it. One day Jennifer's Dad said that he would pay for her lessons and so she could go. Jennifer was really happy and she saved up to buy some dancing shoes.

Then one day there was a dance play and Jennifer was the main character. She was a little grub and she crawled around and buried herself in a big green cocoon. The grub took a long time to change but at last there was a stirring beneath the green material. Very slowly a beautiful butterfly floated out of the cocoon and started to dance around the stage. Everyone thought it was wonderful including Jennifer's Mum who had come to watch the play. The butterfly was not only beautiful but it could do anything it wanted and it danced and danced and danced for ever.

Conclusion

Alexa's family moved two weeks after this session. They moved suddenly and gave no reason. There were rumours that Alexa's mother (who had hardly been out of the house for years) could no longer care for the children and Alexa was moving to live with her father. It is only to be hoped that the support that Alexa had received would be enough to sustain her in her new life.

Supporting exercises and activities

Helping children deal with difficult feelings

Most difficulties arise when a child is unable to externalise their feelings but internalises them to such an extent that when they are no longer containable they erupt in an inappropriate manner. An analogy can be used to explain to children the necessity of allowing difficult feelings to come out before they need to burst out in anger.

The following may be useful:

- Explain to the child that keeping feelings bottled up is like keeping the lid down on a saucepan of boiling pasta. If you keep the lid pressed firmly down, the steam can't escape and eventually the lid will burst off and the water will go everywhere. If you keep lifting the lid every now and again the steam can escape safely.
- Make an 'angry mountain' by using lengths of material. Let the child choose the colours. Let the child hide in the material and remember the feelings of anger. Then allow the child to burst out of the material, exploding the mountain.
- Use a length of old wallpaper. Ask the child to lie down and draw around them. Then using paints or felt-tips, colour in the feelings where they occur in the body.

THE ALIEN MR GIRAFFE

Andrew   Age 9y

Lack of social awareness

Six weekly sessions

The background

Andrew is the only child of fun-loving, tactile but very busy parents. Consequently he has spent a great deal of time on his own playing on his computer or watching, mostly American, cartoon videos. He has also spent many hours in adult company, not having much recourse to children his own age.

He was referred by his teacher and the SENCO following suggestions by the visiting Educational Psychologist that dramatherapeutic intervention might be helpful in the form of social skills, story work etc. Autistic tendencies had been suggested but the brief was not to act upon these suggestions as no diagnosis as such had been made.

The original concern was not so much that Andrew appeared to be failing at school or that he was unhappy but more that his inappropriate and sometimes silly behaviour made him on occasions the butt of his classmates' jokes. The fear was that he would be on the receiving end of much worse than a few jokes when he made the transition to secondary school.

Andrew enjoyed the sessions right from the start. Using mirrors to help with body language and a facial expressions chart to explore appropriate responses some progress was made. As the crux of the situation revolved around communication we then began to work with puppets which facilitated interactive contact.

From the beginning Andrew identified with the yellow-spotted zany-looking Mr Giraffe, leaving me to speak through the sad-faced Mr Clown. This is Andrew's story.

Mr Giraffe didn't come from Planet Earth. He came from a planet very far away called Planet Giraffascope and he knew nothing about Planet Earth. He didn't know anyone at all when he first arrived on Planet Earth but then he made a good friend. His name was Mr Clown. Mr Clown went everywhere with him and taught him all about Planet Earth.

The first thing that Mr Giraffe tried to do was to give Mr Clown a butterfly kiss (brushing his eyelashes against his cheek). Although Mr Clown said that it was very nice he also said that he thought that it wasn't something that you did on Planet Earth especially since Mr Giraffe hardly knew him. Mr Giraffe argued that you could do it at home and Mr Clown said yes but he wasn't at home now and there were certain things which he could do on his planet which if he did on Planet Earth he would be stared at or even laughed at. This made Mr Giraffe stop and think.

How the story was used

We then exchanged puppets and I became Mr Giraffe and Andrew became Mr Clown. Mr Giraffe then proceeded to use the same sort of inappropriate actions and remarks that Andrew tended to use. This was an experiment but Andrew, as Mr Clown, was quick to spot the unsuitable behaviour and took great delight in telling Mr Giraffe about it.

The outcome

We continued the story of Mr Giraffe and Mr Clown over some weeks picking up on all the unsocial and inappropriate behaviour and exploring alternative ways of conducting oneself. In almost every case Andrew, as Mr Clown, was the teacher and I, as Mr Giraffe, the somewhat-recalcitrant pupil. The whole exercise was not so much about teaching Andrew something he did not know as about finding the means of allowing him to remember and confirm something that he did.

After some weeks no more reference was made as to the inappropriateness of Andrew's behaviour. From time to time there was still a 'silly episode' and a falling out with his peers but Andrew was no longer regarded as odd or weird. He had taught himself well.

Supporting exercises and activities

Autism, or Asperger's Syndrome, often manifests itself in a lack of social awareness or social skills. It is, however, difficult to diagnose and should be left to an educational or clinical psychologist.

Lack of socially acceptable behaviour can be due to a number of factors, not least, as in Andrew's case, the lack of siblings or appropriate role models. For an only child any form of attention can be very seductive and Andrew was beginning to thrive on the notice that his 'silly' behaviour was attracting for him.

That Andrew knew how to behave in a socially acceptable manner but was choosing not to was apparent in the Mr Giraffe story. The trick is for the child to feel good enough about himself so that he does not need the inappropriate attention of his peers. By becoming the superior Mr Clown and confirming all that he did know about life, Andrew went some way towards convincing himself that he was 'good enough'.

The following may be helpful in the case of a child who is displaying socially inappropriate behaviour:

- Putting the child in the advisory role of teacher in these circumstances could be helpful if carefully managed so as not to put another child down.
- Using puppets removes the situation one step from real life and provides a sense of safety.
- Before others can accept you, you have to accept yourself. Giving the child some responsibility helps to build his sense of self-esteem instead of allowing him to always play the clown.
- Encourage the child to join a youth club or other extra-curricular activity where he may put into practice what he has learnt.

THE CROWDED HOUSE; THE KIDNAPPING

Natalie   Age 10y

Hearing voices

Twelve weekly sessions

The background

Natalie, aged ten, was the middle child in the family. Her elder sister was much more outgoing and possessed a strong and determined personality. Her younger sister had behavioural problems and took up a lot of her parents' time ever since the death, two years previously, of an auntie to whom she had been very close. The aunt had had special needs and had lived with the family before her death. The parents were sensitive and supportive and were very worried about Natalie when she began to complain that she was hearing voices.

At school Natalie was an achiever although her work had deteriorated a little since the arrival of the voices. In class the teachers said that she was a model pupil, quiet and well mannered who could always be relied on to help or to complete a task. At home her mother told a similar story. Natalie was her helper when the other two were causing problems and demanding attention.

In addition, Natalie's mother explained that she was particularly worried since it appeared that there was a relative in the family who suffered from schizophrenia.

During the first session Natalie told me, without any prompting, about the voices. There were three of them, she said – a man and two ladies. The man's voice was grumpy and frightening and was always telling her to do 'bad things' like punch her friends. One of the ladies was called Juliet and was 32. She was very calm but talked a lot of nonsense saying things like 'helicopter, horse and house'. She had a family and appeared quite normal otherwise, but was always trying to persuade Natalie to put wrong answers down in her work. The last voice again belonged to a woman and she was called Elizabeth. She was 28 and had a very squeaky voice. She also had a baby and was always doing naughty things. Like the man she was constantly exhorting Natalie to punch and kick her classmates.

One of the voices was also good at typing, Natalie volunteered, and together they were always saying things like 'You'll never get rid of us'. The voices came at any time, even in the middle of a lesson. On the whole, they occurred more frequently at school. The only thing which appeared to make them stop was to go and speak to an adult. Natalie was distressed and frightened by the voices and was becoming pale and withdrawn.

Altogether, I worked with Natalie over a period of 12 weeks. After some sessions on trust-building and assessment during which time Natalie gained in self-confidence, it was decided to begin story telling to see if the voices would play any part in the proceedings. Being an imaginative child, story telling came easily to her. She always began by saying what she wanted to tell a story about, dressed up as the main character, told me the parts that I was to play and proceeded to tell and act out the story simultaneously. The following is the first story that Natalie told.

Once upon a time, sometime in the 19th century, there was a princess called Melanie who had a maid called Jasmine. Melanie and Jasmine were unhappy because it was very crowded where they lived and they wanted more space. Eventually they found a house they liked. It was an old-fashioned house. A lady, man and little boy had lived there before and had been very happy. So it was a happy house. Princess Melanie and Jasmine moved in and for two years were very happy.

But then, one day a very bad man who had Alzheimer's came and threw Melanie and Jasmine out of their house. He said that they were all having fun and he wasn't. Melanie and Jasmine found a small cottage where they lived for a year until Melanie's parents found them. When Melanie told her parents what had happened, the man was arrested and thrown into gaol. At first Melanie was worried that he would come back but he didn't and so she was happy.

The outcome

In the week following this story Natalie said that although the voices were still there she didn't feel as scared of them. One, however, had said that he was going to touch her face and he did. This frightened her although apparently it was not done in a nasty way. A visualisation technique was used which focused on clearing the mind using the metaphor of spring cleaning a house since the house was the metaphor Natalie had used herself. Afterwards Natalie drew a picture of her house with the spring-cleaned rooms.

The sessions continued, concentrating on self-esteem-building and on assessment as it was still not clear why Natalie was being troubled. As 'space' was an issue in Natalie's first story it was felt that this was what Natalie needed to allow her to express her difficulties and this was done through the non-directive sessions. In an interview with the mother more light was shed on the situation at home and a theory that Natalie, as the 'good' middle child was somehow over-shadowed and possibly not given enough 'space' by her siblings was considered.

Themes of being kidnapped played a large part in Natalie's story telling. The following is one of them.

Once upon a time there was a family who were moving into a new house. While the Mum and Dad were busy unpacking the little boy and girl ran off to play in the park. They went on the swings and had a great time until suddenly the little girl heard an ice-cream van. The little girl ran off to buy some ice creams and the boy was left alone on the swings.

While he was swinging a man came up to him and asked him if he would help him find his dog. The boy said 'yes' and started to look. But when they got near the man's car, the man pushed the boy inside and drove off. The little girl came back with the ice creams, saw her brother was missing and ran home to tell her Mum and Dad. They called the police and there was a great big search with a helicopter. Eventually the helicopter found the little boy and brought him home. The man had lost his own child and wanted another child of his own. He had to go to prison for five years. The little girl saw the helicopter find her brother and she rang up her Mum to say it was all OK.

The outcome

The theme of kidnapping is a common one in dreams. Although it is not possible to state categorically what each motif in a dream might mean since each dreamer has their own particular dream vocabulary, generally speaking kidnapping is often related to losing an aspect of oneself. In Natalie's case this could possibly be related to loss: not only the loss of her auntie but also the loss of her freedom to act as a child, as she had put herself in the role of the responsible sensible one.

After eight weeks Natalie reported that the voices were not bothering her as much although they were still there. She wasn't as frightened of them and was beginning to be able to stand up to them. Working on the theory that the 'bad' voices still had a message for the 'good' Natalie it was decided to use a fairy tale since fairy tales contain excellent examples of the archetypal 'good and evil'.

Natalie decided to play Snow White, who was her favourite character. After some time of doing this it was then suggested that we reverse roles and she play the evil stepmother. Although it was obvious that this was not a role she was used to Natalie soon became very convincing as the bad queen and obviously enjoyed it.

The final few sessions continued in this way, reversing 'good' and 'bad' roles. We also discussed how Natalie might stand up to the demands of her younger sister and the bossiness of her elder one.

After ten sessions Natalie said that the voices were 'hardly ever there now' and that if they came they didn't bother her at all.

In a final interview, her mother reported that Natalie seemed much happier and much more able to 'stick up for herself'. It was explained that this might well upset the dynamics of the family, and this was understood and accepted.

At the beginning of the following term Natalie reported that the voices had completely disappeared.

Supporting exercises and activities

If schizophrenia is suspected then a referral must obviously be made immediately. As a general rule, however, schizophrenia is usually supported by other changes such as 'a fall-off in work efficiency and a deterioration of behaviour' (Haslam 1990: 29). In Natalie's case, although there had been some deterioration in her work, when she was not being plagued by the 'voices' she was her normal, cheerful self. However, it is always advisable to monitor the situation carefully even if no other signs are present, and to refer if the situation continues. In any case, care must be taken not to be dismissive of the child and his worries.

Natalie was a good example of how important it is to have a functional and viable role system and not become stuck in one particular role (see the section in Chapter 4 on the meaning and value of role play, p. 17). Fairy tales and nursery rhymes can be useful material since they are well known to the child and full of archetypal roles such as the evil stepmother, good fairy and cunning magician. The child can be encouraged to play certain roles and, if appropriate, talk afterwards about how it felt to play that role and which role he felt most comfortable with.

In the case of a child who is complaining of thoughts that go round and round in his head or who appears unable to focus on one activity because of these extraneous thoughts, the following visualisation exercise may be useful. As with any visualisation exercise, care must be taken to keep the activity light and to avoid use of any vocabulary which might suggest dark or danger.

Spring cleaning the mind

- Ask the child to sit comfortably with their feet on the floor.
- Ask him to breathe in deeply through the nose and out through the mouth three times.
- Continue to breathe deeply through the nose and allow the out-breath to become gradually longer (you can count if you like) – for example, breathe in for the count of three and out for the count of five. This will depend on the age of the child.

- Ask the child to imagine a house with five rooms – the room of seeing, the room of hearing, the room of touching, the room of tasting and the room of smelling.
- Ask him to imagine that he is going to one of the rooms. (This can be pre-arranged depending on the situation. In Natalie's case it was the room of hearing.)
- Ask him to imagine that the room is in an awful mess. (He can describe it to you.)
- Then ask him to imagine that he is cleaning it all up, taking out the rubbish, vacuuming it, perhaps even repainting.
- Ask him to describe it to you now.
- Bring the child back slowly to everyday reality by asking him to listen to noises inside the real-life room, to become aware of his breathing and of how he is sitting on the chair, his feet on the floor, and so on.
- You may then like to suggest that the child draws out the room that he has just 'spring cleaned'.

THE BABY TADPOLE

David   Age 6y

Reluctance to grow up

Ongoing support

The background

David was the eldest in his family. At six years of age he already had a younger sister and a baby brother. His younger sister was extremely bright and very quick and the baby showed signs of being the same. David had mild learning difficulties which became more and more apparent with age. His parents were very supportive, but the father, holding down a responsible job himself, had high expectations of David. David's mother, a mild-mannered person, was frequently worn out with looking after three lively children. Control was an issue and one of the complaints of his teachers was that David frequently seemed to take no notice of commands.

David was referred to me by his teacher because of behavioural problems in class and in the playground. In class he would often refuse to do a certain task because he complained it was 'too difficult' or 'he didn't know how'. While it was true that David found some of the work difficult he was becoming reluctant to attempt it even with help. This aversion to work was spilling over to affect even those tasks which were easily within his reach. All David wanted to do was to play.

In the playground David was frequently teased by his classmates because of his babyish manner. He often said he needed help to put on his coat or to do up his shoelaces even though at one point he had been able to do them up perfectly well by himself.

His behaviour at home had deteriorated as well. His mother had complained to the teacher that he had started to bully his younger sister and was becoming unhelpful and disobedient.

I began to work with David primarily on raising his self-esteem. We completed various tasks geared to this and then began to work with story. David loved working with the little figures and although making up stories did not come easily to him, he enjoyed playing with the little animals, moving them around and gradually letting a story unfold. He was especially drawn to a family of frogs comprising two adult frogs, a baby tadpole and two other tadpole/newts in different stages of development. In response to encouraging but not leading questions such as, 'Where did they live?' 'What did they/this one do?' 'What happened then?' David told the following story about his frog family.

Once upon a time there was a family of baby tadpoles and a mummy and daddy frog who lived in a pond near a big house. A little boy and girl lived in the house and they often came to visit the pond to watch the frog family especially the very little tadpoles. 'Oh, aren't they sweet!' they said. 'They're so cute, so little and wriggly,' and the baby tadpoles gave extra wriggles – loving the attention they were getting. They snuggled up close to mummy and daddy frog too and Mummy gave them 'strokes' while Daddy bought them presents.

Tommy was the third-littlest tadpole of all. He loved the 'strokes' and the presents and the nice things the little boy and girl said. He felt he always wanted things to be just as they were, he never wanted anything to change except... he did think it might be rather fun to grow some legs and then maybe some arms like his big brother. Then finally your tail would vanish... poof!... just like that: like his very much older sister.

One day he noticed some bumps on the sides of his body. He felt a bit funny and a bit cross with *everyone, especially with his younger sister who didn't have bumps. To make himself feel better he started playing flicking games with her, only she didn't think it was a game so he got into trouble. Then when he got into trouble Mummy didn't give him 'strokes' anymore and Daddy didn't buy him any presents. He watched his little brother and sister still getting the 'strokes' and the presents and he felt worse.*

The little boy and girl from the big house came down to the pond but they didn't seem to notice him so much – they just kept pointing at the babies and saying how cute they were. Tommy got very cross and a bit scared.

The outcome

David didn't want to finish this story. He said he didn't know what happened next and seemed to get bored with the whole idea. He wanted to continue playing with the tadpoles and having them chase each other in the pond.

How the story was used

In a following session I continued David's story.

One day Tommy found that he could wriggle the strange lumps that he found on the sides of his body. More had appeared further up his body and with the help of these strange lumps he found that he could climb up on things. So he did. He explored all the parts of the pond especially those that he had never been in before. He didn't think so much about the 'strokes' or presents 'cos he was too busy exploring.

One bright sunny morning he wriggled his way to a part of the pond which he had never been to before. Growing up out of the water was an interesting-looking plant. Tommy wriggled and slid and wriggled and slid until finally he was out of the water and high and dry on a lily pad. The surprise nearly made him fall back into the water. For the world didn't end at his pond! He could see lots of green plants and rocks and . . . Tommy's eyes nearly popped out of his head, another pond! Already he could see other frogs hopping around playing games – they were playing leapfrog!

Tommy forgot about everything. He flung back his head and gave an enormous CROOOAAAAAK!!

And then he hopped off to join the frogs in the other pond.

The outcome

At the time of writing, we are in the process of acting out the story of Tommy. The continuation of the story was very much based on the fact that Tommy wanted to grow legs even though he still wanted the 'strokes' from Mummy and the presents from Daddy. Care should be taken when using a continuation story (as has been discussed previously) because the explanation derived by the therapist might be somewhat different to the actual meaning of the child. It is therefore imperative that any continuation story be offered in the first instance to the child only as something that they might like to work with. If no interest is shown then one might surmise that this is not a story which would benefit this particular child.

David has seemed a little more inclined to attempt to do tasks, such as buttoning his coat, for himself. No further complaints about behaviour at home have been received from his mother and David has appeared a little happier in class. The reluctance to grow up, when the safety and seemingly all the rewards of remaining in babyhood appear far more enticing, is an understandable reaction especially when you are hampered by learning difficulties. Unrealistic expectations often result in 'can't' and 'won't' behaviour. Easily achievable targets and goals are a key way forward.

Supporting exercises and activities

When a child's self-esteem has been damaged to the extent that they are refusing to do activities of which they were previously perfectly capable, it is very important not to set up any future scenario where they may fail again. It is necessary to convey the idea that they are valued for who they are and not for who they *could be*.

The following suggestions may be useful for a child such as David.

- Give the child small tasks without too many instructions.
- Find some method of rewarding after completion of each task.
- Read a story, for example from the stories of Winnie-the-Pooh, which focuses on each individual having their contribution to make.
- Direct a class discussion on the subject of valuing people for who they are. Winnie-the-Pooh, the self-declared 'the bear of very little brain' nonetheless has great adventures and solves puzzles.
- Find what interests the child and exploit this through story. In David's case, with his interest in nature, *Wind in the Willows* or *Tales of Beatrix Potter* may capture his imagination.
- Explore the characters in the stories and their unique contributions which may not be about being intelligent.

The background

Johnny was referred through his teacher, because, among other concerns, of his poor attendance record. At any excuse he would be absent from school and when he was in school he appeared isolated and insular. His teacher complained that he avoided eye contact and made little effort to complete his work even when it was explained to him on a one-to-one level. Around school his body language spoke of the victim, shoulders rounded and eyes downcast. He was small for his age and his general demeanour made him appear smaller. He was often the butt of the bullies, never standing up for himself and appeared to have only one friend, a lad named Robin, who often had to answer for him in class.

In an interview with Johnny's mother it was revealed that Johnny had been abused by a friend of the family when he was very little and then again by a next-door neighbour while they were living abroad. The details were sketchy and inconclusive, but Johnny's mother was very worried for him and about the effect that this might have had on him. Although the family had been offered therapy the first time, this had ceased when they moved away and there had been no intervention since they had returned to Britain.

Trust was indeed a major issue for Johnny. During the first few sessions the focus was on building the trust between us. Some self-esteem-building activities were used, including making a shield (p. 46), and some emotional-literacy activities such as the feeling face chart (p. 43) to encourage Johnny to give expression to and externalise what was happening inside him. We also drew a trustline to help Johnny acknowledge his issues of trust and looked at how, why and with whom he had the difficulties.

There were certain issues around the story of the abuse which appeared contradictory, and it was difficult to assess what had happened and, indeed, whether this was the major cause of Johnny's problems. To help with assessment, in the seventh session I asked Johnny if he would like to make up a story about someone, another child. We could make it up as we went along, I said, and see what happened to him or her. Johnny seemed keen on this idea and said that he wanted to make up a story about a boy called David. This is David's story.

David was born in a very large town. He was an only child and he lived with his Mum and Dad.

His Mum worked in a shop. When he was little he was very happy living with his Mum and Dad and going to play school, but when he was five he started ordinary school and that was when he was teased by a gang of boys. David became very sad and then very cross, kind of raging inside. He told his teacher who was called Miss Smith and she told the boys off. Then the teasing stopped.

When David was eight his Mum won the lottery and they decided to go on holiday to America. They ended up living there for one year. There was a boy who lived next door who was a big bully. They all called him Porky and he was 12 years old. Porky teased David and did nasty stuff to him and tricked him. David thought that Porky was his friend. Porky took David to a house where nobody lived.

He told David that there was treasure there. Then Porky started scaring David. David began to get very scared because it was so dark. In the end he told his Mum who told Porky's parents. Then they became friends.

David went back to England, and when he was nine years old he met a nasty boy called Simon who was 13. Simon wasn't nice to David. He tried to beat him up, teased him and called him names.

David told his teacher at school and Simon got into trouble. David and Simon made friends and Simon said he was sorry, but David didn't trust him.

The outcome

It was obvious from Johnny's story that he had major issues with friendship and trust. In class it was apparent that at the same time as wanting friends he was also acting the victim to such an extent that he was manipulating others into hitting him. He was recreating the scenarios to which he was accustomed.

Through puppets we worked on trust and anger issues. We worked through what you did when you were very angry with someone because you felt they had betrayed your trust. The wolf puppet who tried to eat up Johnny's puppet was forgiven and allowed to be friends again. Johnny gradually revealed that in these situations he felt churned up, very tight in his chest, but that he had been told that he had to learn to forgive and be friends because otherwise people wouldn't like him. His anger, however, had to come out in some way and this resulted in winding up his antagonists until they retaliated.

We worked on gradually encouraging and permitting Johnny to feel his anger and allow it to externalise in a safe way. We worked on body language with mirror work, allowing Johnny to become the warrior instead of the wimp. At the same time we built up Johnny's self-esteem by allowing him to 'become' his heroes (James Bond and Bugs Bunny!).

Positive male role models were missing from Johnny's life and 'becoming' a hero, sorting out his own problems rather than allowing older female figures (such as his mother and teachers) to solve them for him was very empowering for Johnny. Bugs Bunny overcame his problems through brains and James Bond through brawn. On more than one occasion when he 'became' James Bond, Johnny used the mirror to see how straight he could stand and how much taller he looked when he put his shoulders back. By his nature and physique Johnny would always be more of a Bugs Bunny than a James Bond but neither character was a victim and both, albeit differently, were in control of their own lives.

The following, when Bugs Bunny met Snake Man, was Johnny's favourite story and he asked to play it through more than once.

Once upon a time Bugs Bunny and his best mate Donald Duck were going for a walk. They started off in the woods and they had a lovely time there, singing and playing. Gradually the trees began to grow thinner and they realised that they weren't in the wood anymore, but they were in a desert. They walked and walked hoping that they would be able to find their way out of the desert, but they couldn't. They were well and truly lost!

They began to feel a bit scared and then suddenly they saw someone coming towards them. It was very hot and they couldn't see properly because there was a kind of shimmer over the sand. They thought it was a man and when he drew near they went up to him to ask him for the way out of the desert. But suddenly they got the *shock of their lives because the man turned into a snake. He slithered down onto the ground and began to wind himself around Donald Duck.*

He was very scary but Bugs Bunny got a big stone and brought it down on the snake man's head. It crushed all his brains and killed him. Afterwards Bugs Bunny and Donald Duck were really happy and they found their way out of the desert.

Conclusion

Gradually teachers noticed that Johnny seemed to have more friends and to be more at ease in the playground. His class teacher commented that he was now able to have eye contact with her and would often put his hand up to ask for help if he didn't understand. Towards the end of the four months of sessions Johnny himself said that he felt better, that he wasn't being bullied in class and that he had lots of friends. We spent the last few sessions rehearsing possible real-life scenarios where Johnny might find himself the victim of bullies and how he might stand up for himself and show by his body language and behaviour that he was no longer a victim.

Supporting exercises and activities

Lifeline

One of the salient features of depression during which the victim role is often adopted is an inability to differentiate between positive and negative. To help children compartmentalise events which have happened to them in their lives and to distinguish between the good and the bad times it may be useful to draw out their life so far in the form of a line, using different colours and drawings or diagrams to represent the highs and lows. It is helpful to remember that if there have been good times in the past then there will be again.

Trustline

When trust is an important issue for a child it sometimes feels as if there is no one they can trust. This is very seldom true and it is helpful to encourage a child to think about the people they can trust even if it is only a little. A line can be drawn and people placed along it in the order in which the child feels they are trustworthy.

Body work

Feeling face chart

For a child who is unaware of the messages that his face is giving to others, using a feeling face chart may be a way into helping him understand that he is often responsible for the way others treat him (see below). An easy introduction is to use the chart as a game, making a face from the chart and then asking the child to guess which one you are making. Afterwards, the child can take a turn.

Mirror work

Similarly, the mirror can be used to show a child the impact his negative feelings are having on his body. Ask the child to feel in his body how it is when he has just been bullied and then let him look in the mirror. Ask him to describe what he sees and if this would be an easy person to bully. Then help him to find the opposite position either by physically doing the opposite or by thinking of a time when someone had given him praise or a reward. Again ask him to describe what he sees and ask if this would be an easy person to bully.

Warrior exercise

Following on from the mirror work exercise, when the child recognises the different messages that his body language is giving out, work can be done by adopting various empowering postures.

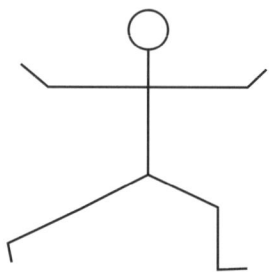

- Raising the fists in a simulation of victory – for example, a goal scored – and exclaiming 'Yes!'
- Adopting the stance of a warrior, feet apart, arms raised to horizontal, front knee bent, head turned to look in direction of forward facing hand, arms and hands firm and strong resembling a spear (see right). This position helps with focus so the child in this position can be asked what they want to happen in their life.

Me and not me story work

Making up a story about a boy or girl about the same age as the child is often a plausible way of allowing the child to explain, through the safety of story, the problems and worries that he himself experiences. Obviously, not everything that happens in the story can be attributed to the child's life, and this method cannot therefore be used as a definitive assessment, but valuable insights can be obtained into what is most important to the child at that particular time.

THE BABY ALIEN	
Tommy	Age 6y
Neglect and abuse, change	
Seven weekly sessions	

The background

Tommy, aged six, was a survivor. This was apparent right from the first time of meeting him. With his cheeky grin and usually cheerful demeanour he gave out the impression of a happy-go-lucky urchin. His invariably optimistic attitude was all the more surprising because it masked a background of neglect and physical and verbal abuse.

Tommy had six brothers and sisters. It was difficult to ascertain whether they were full, half- or step-siblings. His mother and father had split – after an argument in the street, Tommy told me, when the whole neighbourhood had been involved and everyone had cried except for him. His mother often seemed to go away and then Tommy and his younger brother would be looked after by her boyfriend Paul who Tommy didn't like because he 'picked on' him.

Through little figures Tommy told many stories about his background; how he wasn't afraid of anything; how his older brothers and sisters strangled him; how Paul beat him if he didn't get down to the shop in time to buy the bread and milk for breakfast; how his mum was never there and how he didn't care if she was or not, but that he did care about his auntie and uncle. Apparently they often looked after him and he would care very much if they were to go away. He also told me how much he loved his little brother and about the times that he looked after him and kept him out of Paul's way, so that Paul wouldn't beat him up.

It was obvious that Tommy had his own coping strategies many of which centred on denial. Since there was no possibility of affecting any change in his circumstances, the objectives were not to take away Tommy's methods of coping, but to help him become more resilient and self-reliant.

To this end different activities focusing on self-esteem- and self-confidence-building were introduced. Tommy loved the story game which centred on telling stories from various cues extracted at random from different bags. The game involves taking it in turns to throw a dice and move across a board, landing on various spaces entitled – bag of faces, bag of toys, bag of acts or bag of words. These correspond to actual bags with cues inside. The players take it in turns to tell stories based on the cues. The story told by the child can be added to by the therapist to help reframe a particular event or mindset. A story which appears particularly relevant can then be acted out, as was the case with Tommy's story. One of the objects which was pulled out of the 'bag of toys' was a one-eyed alien bug. Tommy told the following story about the baby alien bug.

Once upon a time there was a little boy who had a baby brother. One day this baby brother went off to another planet and his place was taken by an alien. The little boy had to teach the baby alien all about this planet because it was his first time and he didn't know anything. He also had to keep the baby alien away from other people because they might guess he was an alien and hurt him. One day the mother nearly caught the baby alien but the little boy hid him so that the mother couldn't find him and then got him away just in time.

This went on for a while and in the end the baby alien went back to his own planet and the baby brother returned. Tommy, as the baby alien, was asked why he had left his planet in the first place, and he replied that it was because his father shouted at him and was smelly and did things like fart in his face. Even so, he hadn't wanted to leave his planet and he wanted to return because it was fun there.

The outcome

On the seventh session with Tommy he announced on arrival that the family was moving the following day. Sudden family moves and upheavals often happen in this inner-city area, for a number of different reasons. Tommy was his usual cheerful self when discussing the prospect of the move, but there was a note of sadness when he spoke about his friends.

We used the material to create two islands, one of his present home and school and one of his future. Tommy went along with the activity but did not seem very involved. I asked Tommy which was his favourite fairy tale and if he would like to act it out. He chose 'Goldilocks and the Three Bears'. He directed the proceedings and we both played different parts. In Tommy's story the bears became Tommy's closest friends in the end. Having played the story through a couple of times Tommy then announced that he wanted to continue the tale. In his tale Goldilocks moved house and then invited the three bears over to her new house for porridge. We played this story through until Tommy had had enough of it. He went away with his usual big smile.

Although the sessions with Tommy were unfortunately cut short, this final session seemed to end on a positive note in that through his story Tommy showed that he had acquired the resilience to be proactive in a difficult situation, that is by inviting the friends over rather than being miserable alone in the new home. Being Tommy I'm sure that this is exactly what he will do.

Supporting exercises and activities

Self-esteem-building exercises

The shield

- Draw a shield in the child's favourite colour on card or coloured paper.
- Divide it into five sections – two at the top, two in the middle and one at the bottom.
- Give each section a heading, for example:

    What I want to be when I grow up

    Where I want to live

    My friends

    My hobbies *or* What I'm good at

    People who help me.

- Encourage the child to write or draw in each section.
- Cut out the shield and make an arm-piece to enable the child to wear it.

The two islands

- Make two different islands in the room out of material, carpets, cushions or whatever is available.
- Allow the child to think carefully about how he wants these islands to be, for example what shape and colour, as they represent the present and the future.

- Invite the child to sit on the 'present' island and talk about how he feels sitting there, the good and bad feelings. Ask him to look across at the 'future' island and tell you how that feels.
- When he is ready ask him if he would like to go across to the 'future' island, and how he wants to go – for example, by boat, stepping stones or walking on water!
- Ask him if there is someone or something he would like to take with him from the 'present' island to help with the transition.
- In his own time allow the child to make the transition.
- Sit on the 'future' island and ask the child how that feels.
- Ask the child how it feels looking back at the 'present' island.
- Praise him for having made the transition.

N.B. This exercise can be helpful during primary/secondary school transition and enforced-parting change.

THE INDIAN GIRL

Charlene   Age 6y

Lack of self-confidence and speech defects

Eight weekly sessions and ongoing intermittent support

The background

Charlene, at six, was the youngest of a family with six children some of whom were half- brothers or -sisters. Family life had been unstable for Charlene with many changes of accommodation and mother or father's partners. She lacked self-confidence, and often had friendship problems and difficulties with hearing. In addition she stuttered, at times so badly that it was difficult to hear what she was trying to say. She had a general air of nervousness which seemed to overcome her completely at times. Her academic ability was low and the expectation was that she would not find the medium of story telling at all easy.

This, however, proved to be completely inaccurate. It soon became very clear that Charlene possessed an extremely lively imagination and was able to use projection very easily. In addition she was good at sequencing and some of her stories held twists and turns which she was able to remember in subsequent sessions. It became clear that Charlene often escaped into the world of fairy tale to avoid confronting the reality of the world around her.

Charlene liked working best with the lengths of brightly coloured material. She was enthusiastic about dressing herself up and about decorating the room although it was not always obvious exactly what she had in mind. As she played she would often chatter away to herself and switch randomly from one theme to the other. After some sessions of passively witnessing her play it became obvious that the theme of mothers and babies played a central part as did the occurrence of talking to a baby in another language.

In a subsequent session I asked her who she was and where she lived. This is the story she told.

Once upon a time there was a girl and she lived in India. She had a baby and she loved the baby very much. Every day she changed the baby's nappy and she fed the baby and she talked to it all day long in the Indian language and the baby understood everything she said. She also looked after her mother and father. What nobody knew was that this girl was Supergirl in disguise. Everyone thought that she was just an Indian girl with a baby but at night she changed into Supergirl and she could fly. She flew everywhere – all around the world.

One day some bad men came and took away her mummy and daddy. All day long she looked after her baby and talked to it, but that night she changed into Supergirl and she flew all round the world looking for them. Then she found them. They were very cold and hungry and they were really pleased to see her.

She saved them and took them home back to her baby. They didn't mind that she was Supergirl and said that they had known that she was all the time. They all lived happily ever after with the baby.

How the story was used

The sense of empowerment which Charlene gained from acting through this story was tangible. What was also very noticeable was that when she was speaking to the baby in the 'Indian' language, there was no trace of a stutter. Although completely unintelligible, her sentences were flowing and easy. She seemed completely at home with this 'foreign language'.

Over a number of sessions Charlene continued to play through the story of the Indian girl who became Supergirl with a number of different twists and turns. There was always a baby in the story and Supergirl always saved someone or something. Charlene was living through her fantasies of being strong, a carer and possessed of superhuman powers including that of speaking fluently in a 'foreign' tongue. By acting through her dreams Charlene was receiving a glimpse of what it might be like to achieve the impossible, including that of speaking intelligibly. To her, English might well have seemed a 'foreign language'.

I was not asked to take part in any of the stories but remained as witness to them. As it became apparent to Charlene that she was 'allowed' to speak in this strange language and that she was not going to be laughed at or interrupted, so her speech became clearer and her sentences longer and more flowing. Indeed, there were times when it almost seemed as if she were actually speaking a language of which I had no knowledge!

The outcome

Over a period of a few months Charlene's confidence began to improve. Sessions were held on a more intermittent basis. Charlene began to work with a speech therapist, and with the combined input of the speech and drama therapy her speech started to become clearer with less evidence of a stutter. At times of family upheaval she reverted to the original state of nervousness but appeared to be more easily able to regain her confidence when things had settled down again.

Supporting exercises and activities

N.B. Concerns over speech defects should in the first instance be referred to a speech and language therapist.

In some sporting activities, coaches work with the effects of visualisation on improving performance. Being able to visualise yourself achieving something has been proved to have a beneficial effect on the eventual outcome. This was the case with Charlene. Being able to visualise herself and, indeed, taking it a step further and actually acting 'as if' she were strong, empowered, in a position to rescue and nurture others as well as fluent and articulate brought the impossible a little nearer realisation.

Empowerment through dramatherapy for children suffering from loss of control in their lives is discussed in Chapter 4, 'The Value of Personal Story Telling'. However, allowing a child who has a nervous speech defect such as a stutter to speak and to tell stories in a nonsensical tongue may be of help in overcoming the feelings of inadequacy that normal language communication may cause. Swapping to the nonsensical language activates the creative, right brain and switches off the logical left brain which strives to make sense of it all. Thus freed from the necessity to 'make sense' the child can relax and the language can flow.

Games for speaking and listening in groups

Talking in numbers

In pairs, think of a situation and discuss it using only numbers – for example, an argument, a request, an enquiry. The scene can be acted out. The rest of the group try to say what they think is going on.

One-word stories

With a partner, practise taking it in turns to say a word or phrase to make up a story. You can act this out as you go.

Lawyers

Group stands in a circle with one member in the centre. The one in the centre is the lawyer. The lawyer asks questions, but the person being asked must not answer, the one to his left answers for him. If the person being asked answers, he is out. Likewise if the person to the left fails to answer, he is out too. New rules can be added to the game, for example 'You must not answer yes or no'. The game can also be speeded up to continue around the circle or change direction within the circle.

Voice work

Group yell

In a circle, start bending down making low sound. As the group moves to an upright position, the sound increases to very loud when on tiptoe and then decreases as they bend down again.

Throw the ball

Throw the ball to a partner. Start very near to each other and make a sound or say a word. As the pair separate, the sound becomes louder and as they draw near to each other again it becomes softer.

Sound wall

The group stands in a circle. All take a deep breath and make same sound – for example, 'aah'. Individuals take another breath and repeat sound when necessary.

THE NASTY ALIENS; RETAKILL AND HAPPYLANDS

Christie   Age 9y

Family dynamics

Six weekly sessions

The background

Christie, age nine, was referred through her teacher following conversations with Christie's mother. Her mother was concerned that Christie, from being a naturally lively and happy child, had begun to have nightmares which resulted in her becoming withdrawn and preoccupied. Her work was beginning to deteriorate and her usual cheerful smile was missing from the classroom. In addition, at home she had begun to pick fights with her older brothers, teasing them until they retaliated.

Christie was a bright, intelligent girl, and at first there seemed to be no obvious reason for the nightmares, which had also resulted on occasions in her calling out in her sleep and sleepwalking. At nine she was reaching the age when final separation from parents becomes a necessity and any unresolved attachment issues often begin to emerge. This did not appear to be the case with Christie.

In addition there did not appear to be any particular family problems which could be disturbing her, neither had there been any recent family bereavement or difficulties with her peer group. Nevertheless, her nightmares, although not frequent, were powerful enough to wake Christie and prevent her from being able to go back to sleep in her own bed, thus proving a disturbance to other members of the family.

On discussion with her teachers it was discovered that Christie often hid her feelings behind her bright smile. She would continue to smile even when being told off. Something in Christie was being masked.

As the nightmares appeared to be central to Christie's problems, we began by discussing how they made her feel and how much detail she remembered. Although they varied a little, they had a common theme and evoked a common feeling of powerlessness.

The following is the major theme of Christie's dreams.

I am asleep in my bed and suddenly I hear a noise. The noise is coming from the toy box in the corner of the room. I wake up and see two nasty-looking aliens climbing out of the box. They come over to the bed and stand beside me. They look really scary and I know they are going to attack me.

They come over to the bed and they begin to poke me with sticks. Then one of them takes a pillow

And he puts it over my face. I think he is going to smother me. Then I wake up.

How the dream was used

Christie was very happy to act out her dream. She directed the proceedings and told me, as the aliens, where to stand and what to do. She then became the aliens and, as Christie, I asked her why she was behaving in this way. Christie, as the aliens, answered that it was because they didn't like her (Christie's) face – she had an evil face.

After we had de-roled I asked Christie to look in the mirror and tell me what she saw. She admitted that she saw a pretty face with no trace of evil. I then asked her if anyone had ever told her that they didn't like her face. She said her brothers had said this on more than one occasion.

Christie was keen to play through the dream again and change the ending. Her idea was to get up out of bed and face the aliens telling them to go away in a voice which had to be obeyed. This she did, asking to play it through more than once.

The outcome of the dream

Christie had no more bad dreams and no more incidences of sleepwalking from this time on. She still, however, was extremely reluctant to sleep in her own bed. In an interview with Christie's mother, Christie agreed to stop teasing her brothers and her mother agreed to have a word with the boys about their 'rough play'. Things began to improve but were still not quite right. In one session Christie told stories about the good and bad part of her mind and that she was scared that if she slept alone the bad part of her mind would come at her with a knife. We chose little figures for the good and bad parts of her mind and she gave them names: Retakill for the bad part and Happylands for the good. This is the story she then told about them.

Once upon a time a little girl was sleeping alone in her bed. One night when she was asleep Retakill crept out of the cupboard and came at her with a knife. He stood over the bed and the little girl was very frightened. She called out for help but nobody came. She got more and more scared because she thought that Retakill was going to kill her. She could see his knife even though it was dark. She screamed again and then out of the same cupboard came Happylands. He was bigger than Retakill so it wasn't hard for him to fight Retakill. Eventually, after a fight, Happyland won and he threw Retakill out. The little girl went back to sleep.

The conclusion

Gradually, over a few weeks, Christie's confidence increased until she was spending more and more time in her own bed. At the beginning of the following term Christie came running up to me with a big smile and announced proudly that she was sleeping in her own bed all the time now and that everything was really good. She showed me the thumbs up to describe how she felt – absolutely at the top!

Supporting exercises and activities

Enactment of dreams, especially nightmares, should not be undertaken unless by a trained therapist to avoid the possibility of retraumatisation. More information on dreams and sleepwalking is given in Chapter 6 'Dream Work'. Many children are frightened by the odd dream, but if a child is constantly frightened by a recurring nightmare, and in the absence of a trained therapist, the following may be helpful:

- Ask the child what kind of feelings the dream leaves him with.
- Ask him to point to the part of the body where he feels these feelings, for example:
  - Is it the throat? Is he trying to communicate something and can't?

- Is it the solar plexus? Is he suffering from feelings of loss of identity, lack of self-confidence?
- Is it the stomach or heart? Is he overanxious or fearful?
- Is it the head? Is he trapped in his head and unable to express how he feels in the rest of his body?

N.B. The above are only guidelines and do not necessarily apply in every case.

• Ask the child if something is happening in his life at the moment which reminds him of these feelings. (There should obviously be an awareness of child protection issues and procedures before work of this kind is undertaken.)

N.B. Very often, once the dream material has been brought from the subconscious into the conscious – once it has been 'spotted', so to speak – its job is done and the nightmares will cease.

THE POINTED DIAMOND

Douglas   Age 8

Parental neglect

Nine weekly sessions and ongoing support

The background

Douglas was the eldest child of a very young mother who had gone on to have three other children by three different fathers. Although loved, Douglas was given very little time and attention and was allowed to roam the streets with his friends until well after dark. He was frequently caught and brought home by the police having been involved in some slightly dubious activity. He was a well-meaning, kind child who knew the difference between right and wrong but needed constant reminders. He was slow to form relationships, particularly with adult males, and hated any form of change. Class changeovers from one male teacher to another were therefore a time of great difficulty for Douglas.

Douglas was referred by his teacher as having big problems in class shortly after the start of the new term. The behaviour problems had been simmering for a while but had been managed the previous term by his teacher and some therapeutic intervention. The mother was expecting another baby and there was some fear around this for Douglas since she had experienced a miscarriage some time previously and had ended up in hospital. Douglas was reacting by behaving in a sullen way and having anger outbursts at the slightest provocation.

Douglas picked up easily from where he was with the previous work. At first he had proclaimed that he was 'no good' at story telling. His self-esteem had always been fragile and was now at an all-time low. Gentle but persistent encouragement and praise, no matter how short the story, began to give Douglas some faith in his own powers. Soon he was telling long stories and revelling in this new-found skill, which also gave him the freedom to explore his fragmented and unstable background. This is one of his stories.

Once upon a time there was a little boy called David. There was one thing in the world which David had always wanted and that was a special diamond stone which he had seen in a shop near their house. Their family often didn't have very much money and David knew that his mum would never be able to afford this stone which seemed quite magical to him.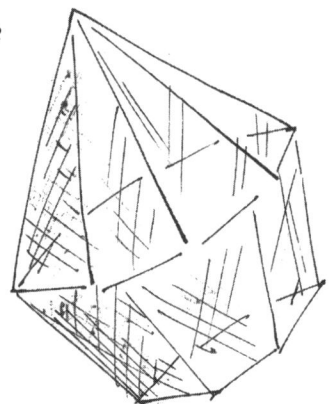

His mum often sent him down to the shop to buy things that she'd forgotten – a pint of milk, some potatoes or some cereal for breakfast. Always when he went past the diamond shop he peered in the window to make sure that his special stone was still there.

Also David was allowed to do pretty much what he liked and he always played out on his bike, sometimes until quite late at night. Occasionally he got into trouble for this from his mum or his mum's boyfriend, but mostly he got away with it and he always came home past the diamond shop just to check that his stone was still there.

One day David got the biggest shock of his life.

He'd come home early for once. He was fed up 'cos his mates were playing cherry-knocking – knocking on the doors of old people's houses and running away. David didn't really like the game.

And the first thing he saw when he came in was a big cardboard box on the kitchen table. And inside the box . . . was the diamond! It threw rainbows all around the kitchen.

David picked up the diamond. His Mum was sitting at the table, but she didn't say anything. David held the diamond up to the light. He could see another land in the glass. He held it to his chest and its point pierced his heart. It went right through like a dagger. David died.

How the story was used

Douglas told this story following a 'bad day' although he didn't say why it was bad. A suggestion that it be acted out was met with enthusiasm. Douglas wanted me to play the part of the mum and after he, as David, had died, he was most insistent that I was to be really, really upset. He left me 'crying' for a long time and then he told me that I should have a cup of tea. Then I had to bury him and cry again and then have another cup of tea. This part of the story took a long time and was by far the major part of the session.

The outcome

This is only one of many stories that Douglas told but is the most poignant and as such deserves, I feel, to stand alone without attempts at interpretation. What or who the diamond symbolises is open to discussion, but perhaps only Douglas himself really knows. Suffice it to say that Douglas derived great satisfaction from seeing me, as the mother, crying at his deathbed.

Support is continuing for Douglas since his is one of those situations which nothing and no one can 'fix', but one hopes that something might help 'manage'.

This kind of support appears to help Douglas in that he is much worse without it. When life at home is uneventful he blossoms and, to a degree, he is learning to become less affected by its instability. For a child who proclaimed he was 'no good' at stories, the depth of feeling and imagination portrayed in this story stands as testimonial to his development.

Supporting exercises and activities

Moral dilemmas

In the case of a child like Douglas who knows the difference between right and wrong but needs confirmation in the absence of consistent role models, a suggested activity might be to read or tell the story of 'Dick Whittington'. The scene where Dick is faced with a choice could be played through and a class discussion held on such moral dilemmas. The child in question may then benefit from playing the part of Dick and experiencing how it feels to make a difficult choice, stand up for himself and believe in justice which turns out well in the end.

Self-esteem-building exercises

The shield

This activity is explained in Tommy's story (see p. 46).

Family and friends

- Using a collection of small figures, animals or people, ask the child to choose one to represent himself.

- Then ask him to choose one each to represent each person in his close family, extended family and friendship group. Other significant people can be added, such as teachers and group leaders.
- Place the object representing the child at the centre and ask the child to arrange the other chosen objects around it, putting them as close or as far away as he wishes.
- Comment on how much support the child has around him.
- If wished, the child can then move certain objects closer or further away depending on how he would like things to be.
- Draw out the arrangement putting the child in the centre and using coloured pens to connect the child to his family and friends.

Anger-management exercises

Breathing exercises can be very useful in dealing with uncontrolled anger. With small children visualisation is helpful.

The candle

- Ask the child to hold a forefinger up in front of his face and pretend it's a candle.
- Ask him to take a deep breath and blow softly on the tip so as not to put the flame out.
- Ask him to take as long as possible breathing out which means taking as deep as possible a breath in.

Gorilla breath

This is a version of alternate-nostril breathing but again visualisation is helpful.

- Ask the child to close his right nostril with his right forefinger and breathe in through his left nostril.
- Stop the left nostril with the left forefinger and breathe out through the right.
- Repeat breathing in through the right and stopping the left.
- If the arms are swung as each nostril is stopped in turn this can imitate the swinging arms of a gorilla.

The woodcutter

- Ask the child to imagine he has an axe and to take hold of it with both hands.
- Ask him to imagine a huge trunk of a tree which he is going to chop into small logs.
- Ask him to take a really deep breath and to raise the axe above his head.
- As he brings it down to chop the logs he breathes out sharply.
- After twenty 'chops' the child usually feels less angry.

THE RED AND ORANGE MONSTER

Stacey   Age 12y

Overprotection

Ten weekly sessions

The background

Stacey, age 12, lived alone with her mother, her father having died two years previously. She was in her first year at secondary school and by the spring term, concern was expressed over her inability to 'fit in' with her tutor group. She appeared to have no real friends, was occasionally the victim of bullies and was often absent from school, her mother telephoning or writing to say that Stacey did not 'feel well'.

The mother would often appear at the start of school to explain to Stacey's tutor how difficult it was for Stacey since her father had died and how much she worried about her. The mother always brought Stacey to school herself although they only lived a few doors away. At lunchtimes Stacey would either go home for lunch or ring her mother.

It was felt by the school that this mutual need was not doing either Stacey or her mother any good, but that the break would have to come from Stacey as there was obviously some difficulty in involving the mother. The situation came to a head at the end of Stacey's first term at school when Stacey herself volunteered to her tutor that she didn't think she had settled in to school at all well.

The previous sessions

Stacey was invited to join a dramatherapy group which comprised two girls and six boys from her year who had been selected by their year head following concerns about their settling in to the new school.

She came along to the first session somewhat reluctantly and although smiling constantly was very quiet and shy throughout the hour. She established an immediate rapport with the only other girl in the group and appeared to be very wary of the six boys. For the second session she was absent but legitimately ill.

During the third session Stacey began shyly to volunteer. Only five out of the eight children were present and it so happened that three of the noisier boys were away. In the short 'talking time' which was held every session when the children aired any problems or discussed the 'best and worst thing' which had happened in the week, the discussion centred around situations that might happen at school. Encouraged by the participation and openness of the other children, Stacey volunteered a situation which she said 'might' happen when a child was too scared to tell her teacher that she did not understand because she had been 'told off' before by this teacher for not completing homework.

Using the group as the teacher and the rest of the class Stacey showed us what 'might' happen to some fictitious child, and using sculpts and stills and role play we then rehearsed different ways in which this child might deal with the situation. The permission to pretend that this was a situation which had happened to another child gave Stacey the safety she needed and only once did she forget and say 'I'.

During the fourth, fifth and sixth sessions the group began to go through its storming period (see Chapter 8 'Group Work'). Previous work done with Stacey had empowered her to the extent that she felt confident enough to scold those boys whom she felt were misbehaving. She was also helped in this by the fact that she was able to do it 'in role'.

In a scene where the group had to escape from a hut in the jungle and traverse swamps, deserts and other dangers, Stacey, in her role of a mother with no husband and one child (a role obviously dear to her heart) was able to become quite incensed with her fellow travellers who she felt were endangering the safety of her child by their behaviour. This was a new role for Stacey who was at risk of becoming stuck in her role of 'the nurtured one' (see Chapter 3, 'The Significance of Metaphor and Symbol in Dramatherapy').

During the sixth session, work on the children's own personal stories began. The work centred on the six-part storyboard technique explored by Alida Gersie and Mooli Lahad (see Chapter 4, 'The Value of Personal Story Telling'). The session began with a period of relaxation and then a guided visualisation in which the children were invited to imagine a place, a landscape – anywhere they liked – and put themselves in this landscape. They were then to imagine they were on a mission, and they might, if they wished, have someone to help them on their way. Somewhere on their journey they were to come face to face with a powerful monster with whom they struggled and whom they eventually overcame.

After the visualisation the children drew their monsters, landscapes and helpmates.

Stacey took a long time over the drawing of her monster and the landscape which was reminiscent of a desert. Her helpmate was a round, fat, somewhat motherly figure! The following three sessions were spent in an enactment of each of the children's stories culminating in the slaying of their monster. The child to whom the story belonged was the 'director' and could organise the group as he or she wished. In order for the monster to be as frightening as possible, the whole group (apart from the child whose story it was) became the monster. Using all sorts of material, body shapes and noises, these monsters became quite lifelike. When the time came for Stacey to be the 'director' of her own story, she never hesitated. It began in the desert she said, and she used yellow material to depict the sand, then she took much time and trouble to arrange the various bits of green and brown material which became the stunted trees. The following is her story.

Once upon a time there was a girl who was travelling through a dried-up desert. There was no water and even the trees had shrivelled up becoming just green and brown stumps.

The girl had a friend with her who was there to help her. She had to get through the desert because she was on a mission to find the treasure that had been lost and that belonged to the nearby town. The townspeople hadn't been able to come out and look because there was a big monster lurking around in the desert.

Suddenly from behind one of the trees there sprang a huge multi-headed red and orange monster which snarled ferociously. At first the girl was scared but she fought valiantly and finally overcame the monster with the help of her friend. But the monster wasn't properly dead. The girl knew that the only way she would really get rid of the monster once and for all was if she stood up to it all by herself. It was a big decision to make – to cross the desert all by herself knowing that the monster was lying in wait for her.

Finally she agreed to do it. This time the monster snarled even more ferociously and seemed to take a very long time to die. But finally it gave its last roar and the girl stood over it with her sword poised.

All the townspeople came rushing out to see and were so grateful that at long last the big monster had been destroyed and they could get their treasure back that they carried the girl around the town, put her on a special throne and all bowed to her.

The outcome

Stacey was much empowered by this enactment. It is Alida Gersie who considers the nature of the helpmate as the most likely area of healing for the client, but in Stacey's case it was the decision to cope alone, without a helpmate which seemed to be the source of her empowerment.

In the final session before Easter a story bag was passed around. Each child, now used to thinking spontaneously, said which story they thought was in the bag. Together as a group we then made up a story with each child adding his or her own original suggestion. We echoed the suggestion and copied the child's suggested action for the new character or element, thus giving the whole structure the feeling of ritual. Rituals have an important place during periods of transition (see Chapter 4, 'The Value of Personal Story Telling') and, this being the last session, it heralded the transition back to their normal classes.

Within this safe and structured framework the children were asked which bits of the story they liked best, which bit, perhaps, they would like to take away with them. Stacey chose the tidal wave. As the group watched, she 'became' the tidal wave, growing larger and larger as she rushed round and round the room before collapsing in a heap of exhaustion on the floor. 'I swamped you, all of you,' she said and grinned happily.

Stacey returned to her tutor group quietly cheerful. With the onset of the new term some anxiety returned. Her mother, however, no longer came up before school and gradually, with her tutor's help, Stacey began to join clubs at lunchtime which meant that she no longer had the time to phone her mother. Her tutors and teachers commented on the change in her. The last time I saw her she was hurtling down a corridor with her best friend chattering non-stop about their latest adventure until she was pulled up short by her year head. 'Stacey,' he said, 'Whatever has got in to you?'

Whatever it is – it is to be hoped it is there to stay.

Supporting exercises and activities

Ideas for working with groups can be found in Chapter 8, 'Group Work'.

THE QUEEN WHO SHOUTED

Sophie and Amber   Age 8y

Learnt behaviour

Eight weekly sessions

The background

Sophie and Amber, both aged eight, were referred by their teacher following concerns over their behaviour in class and in the playground. Both girls showed signs of being precocious, extremely streetwise and prematurely aware. In addition they were both often very nasty to the other girls in the class, forming power struggles and control groups by their behaviour. Although not overt bullies, they were succeeding in upsetting many of the gentler members of their peer group. It appeared that Sophie was also being bullied outside school by a much older and in her mother's words 'rougher' girl.

At first the work centred around role models, good and bad, and how the girls wanted to be when they had grown up. It was obvious that both girls had been exposed to much adult behaviour both in terms of language and activities. Without any judgemental intervention the sessions were concerned with allowing the girls to form their own opinions of the appropriateness of certain behaviours by acting out and following scenarios through to their natural conclusion.

At the end of each session a short discussion was held during which the girls were encouraged to comment on the outcomes and to look at alternative behaviours. In subsequent weeks the alternative behaviour patterns were enacted with the various different conclusions. The conclusion as to whether certain behaviour was desirable or not was always left up to the child to decide.

After a series of ten sessions it was decided that the girls might make up their own play together for me to watch as the audience. They loved decorating the Rainbow Room with the material and took a long time dressing up as the twin princesses. This is their play.

Once upon a time there were two princesses who lived with their mother, the Queen, in a big castle. Although they were very happy dressing up and playing in the castle they were not happy when the Queen shouted at them. She did this very often. And the more she shouted the more unhappy the princesses became.

Finally, one day they decided to run away. They put on their best clothes and packed a lunch and ran away into the forest. The forest was very big and dark and the two princesses were very scared. They wandered around trying to find a place where they might sleep. Everything seemed huge and very scary and as if there were monsters behind every tree. They were nearly in tears when suddenly they heard a funny croaking noise. They looked down and there, near a pond, was a big, fat frog. One of the princesses bent down and picked it up because she felt sorry for it. The other princess said she ought to kiss it because that's what you did in stories. They neither of them wanted to, but finally the first princess kissed the frog and, of course, he turned into a prince.

They went back to the castle with the prince but the Queen was very angry. She shouted at them more than ever and said that they couldn't stay with the prince and that the prince had to leave. At first the princesses were scared of their mother but then, because they loved the prince, they decided that they would leave with him. They told their mother that she could shout all she liked but they were going. And they did.

And they lived happily ever after.

The outcome

This was the last session the girls had together. After the summer break the teacher reported that both girls had greatly improved. They were both more subdued and much gentler with their peer group. Amber had even volunteered to look after a new girl in their class. Both girls were beginning to reap the rewards of positive behaviour and it felt as if they had discovered that they had choices in life. It was concluded that for the time being the sessions could cease but that the girls would be monitored in case there was a return to the previous behaviour.

Supporting exercises and activities

Although problems of 'learnt behaviour' can be tackled through cognitive behaviourist strategies and reinforcement of suitable role models, it is, as previously stated, in the 'doing of a thing' that it is remembered.

Miller (1983: 189) says that 'a common set of learning principles underlies both normal and abnormal behaviour' and there is a need therefore 'to change the reinforcement contingencies so that desirable behaviour is reinforced and thereby maintained, while undesirable behaviour is ignored and thereby weakened'.

With these two principles in mind it can be seen that dramatherapy and the acting out of the desirable behavioural model is an optimum way of reinforcing and maintaining the positive outcome. The girls, however, had first to decide exactly what was the desirable behaviour and then to learn to say 'no' to the undesirable.

Games and exercises to help positive-role-model reinforcement are as follows:

Role awareness

- Draw a diagram with the child putting a circle with the word 'me' inside to represent the child.
- Draw lines from the circle to end in other circles denoting the different roles the child plays, such as child, friend, grandchild and so on.
- Do the same for the mother/father etc. as appropriate. (For example, draw another circle and write the name of the mother in the centre. Then draw lines to other circles showing the other roles the mother plays.)
- Discuss how it is sometimes difficult to be the same person and yet play all these roles.
- Talk/act out from the diagrams how the mother behaves towards her daughter and then how she behaves towards her husband etc.

The objective is to look at what is appropriate behaviour in each different role. Children often regard their mother and father as only having one role, in other words, the role of parent.

Positive and negative roles

- Place two chairs a small distance apart.
- Explain to the child that one is where the well-behaved or positive mother/father, daughter/son sits and the other is where the badly behaved or negative one sits.
- Ask the child to sit in each in turn and act out the different behaviours.
- Discuss which they prefer and why.

Scenarios

- Think of a situation – for example, a child spilling his milk at breakfast – and act out negative and then positive reactions.
- Extend both reactions to a logical conclusion.
- Discuss the outcomes.
- Talk about which reaction is more helpful and why.

THE STONE OF LIFE; THE TWO ISLANDS

Sarah   Age 8y

Attachment

Six weekly sessions

The background

Sarah was referred by the classroom assistant after a discussion with her mother. Sarah's mother had experienced difficulty in disengaging herself from her daughter at school in the morning. Sarah, although eight years old, would cling on to her mother's arm trying to find all sorts of excuses to prevent her mother from leaving the classroom and would finally resort to tears, an embarrassment both to herself and her mother. In addition to this, Sarah was refusing to go to sleep at night unless her mother remained at her bedside. Only once Sarah was asleep could her mother leave the room. Sometimes this took up to two hours and Sarah's mother, although a caring, loving mother, was beginning to find the whole process very wearying. Sarah's teacher also reported that her work was not up to its usual standard and that she was inclined to burst into tears at the slightest criticism or provocation, tiredness being one of the issues.

Sarah's older brother had not had any similar problems and had always done very well at school. The children had a nurturing close family background and there appeared to be no obvious reason why these problems had suddenly arisen.

Sarah was a bright, intelligent girl with a good imagination, and from the first she loved this way of working. Being endowed with a lively imagination also meant that she was somewhat of a worrier and it soon became clear that she had an underlying anxiety. Her mother had two miscarriages somewhere between the births of Sarah and her brother. Sarah was worried that somehow, someday she too might die.

The first step was to involve Sarah and her mother in a discussion in which Sarah could find out more about what had happened. She needed to understand that this was a sad but not infrequent happening and certainly not an event particular to her family that was a harbinger of doom as her fears were telling her. Sarah had also had a dream which had occurred on more than one occasion and which was part of the reason why she was reluctant to go to sleep at night. The following is her dream.

I was walking along a road all by myself. There were trees and flowers and birds and the sun was shining. Suddenly a kind of green thing popped up out of the hedge and said I had to hurry up and go across the next field to get this stone. It was very important because it was the stone of life. So I ran but it was really difficult and my legs wouldn't move very fast. In the field there was a swing and I went to sit on it. I was swinging away and then I remembered the stone. I got near to the stone and I was just about to get hold of it and these monster-like creatures, kind of like aliens, jumped out at me and took the stone. They said I couldn't have it. I tried to take it off them but I couldn't. They pushed me away and they laughed at me. I felt really panicky and then I woke up.

How the dream was used

The first suggestion to help Sarah feel protected at night was to buy a dreamcatcher (see p. 65). She hung this over her bed and was somewhat reassured. It did not, however, deal with the reason why she was having the dreams and to this end we decided to act out the dream, with Sarah being herself and me being the monsters. Coincidentally, there happened to be a large stone which was being used as a doorstop in the room we were using which made an excellent stone of life!

Having acted out the dream exactly as it was remembered, Sarah was then asked if she would like the ending to be different and, if so, how. She wanted to be able to seize the stone from the alien monsters and take it back and sit on the swing. So this scene was then acted out three or four times until Sarah felt it was enough.

The following week Sarah drew out her dream with herself holding the stone.

The outcome

From that time on, the situation began slowly to improve. It was suggested that a stone symbolic of the stone of life be bought for Sarah and a 'tiger's eye' crystal, which is said to have the properties of protection, was acquired. Sarah was able to go to sleep clutching this.

Although much better, Sarah still had difficulty in going to sleep without her mother. Further work in addition to some firm boundary-setting was obviously needed. While Sarah's mother worked with a clock, gradually shortening the time she would be prepared to sit with her, I worked on understanding the reason behind the continuing attachment.

In discussion with Sarah's mother it was discovered that Sarah had never been quite 'right', had been more clingy and nervous ever since she had been lost in a big supermarket store a few months previously. Sarah's favourite character happened to be Little Red Riding Hood and we spent some sessions getting lost in the woods and asking directions from the animals, not panicking and finding our own way out. In addition to this, we explored the original scene and discovered that it wasn't that mum had disappeared or got lost, but that Sarah had simply wandered away.

Sarah continued to improve and it was decided the time had come to approach the issue of a complete separation from mother. The following enactment, once it had been set up from different materials decided by Sarah, was again wholly directed by Sarah herself.

Once upon a time there were two islands – a baby island and a grown-up island. The baby island was all pink and white and the grown-up island was deep purple and maroon. They were in the middle of a sparking blue and green sea. Sarah and her friend went to sit on the baby island. They talked about how they felt sitting on the baby island and how it felt looking across to the grown-up island knowing that they would go there some day.

When they felt ready they decided to go across to the grown-up island so they put some stepping stones across the sea and carefully made their way across. They talked about how it felt sitting on this island, and Sarah said how she was surprised that it felt better. She said she had felt a bit lost on the baby island. They talked about what Sarah would do if ever she got lost on the grown-up island and Sarah had lots of ideas.

Then they talked about the feelings of being lost and Sarah thought that they belonged to the baby island. She wanted to take them back and bury them on the baby island. So they did. Then they returned to the grown-up island. Then Sarah had a wonderful idea about how to stop the feelings ever returning.

She threw away the stepping stones.

Conclusion

The following week Sarah's mother greeted me with a smile. Sarah was content to go to sleep with her mother only remaining in the room for five minutes. Some weeks down the line Sarah no longer even needed this support and went off to bed and to school quite happily on her own.

Supporting exercises and activities

Attachment issues where children find difficulty in separating from parents, usually mothers are surprisingly common and may arise for a number of reasons. The best known research on attachment has been done by J. Bowlby in his book Attachment and Loss (1969). In the case of Sarah, coming as she did from a loving and well-intentioned family, the presenting problems although distressing, were not life-changing. In some severe cases of attachment the results may be much more disturbing.

As already mentioned, it is not suggested that enactment of dreams be undertaken unless by a trained therapist for fear of retraumatisation. However, the following are a few ideas which may help.

- Dreamcatchers are readily available in shops and appear to have some effect on some children. Dreamcatchers originate from Native American customs and are circles of wood or cane to which interwoven thread in the shape of a net has been attached. This 'catches' the dreams. Beads, feathers and shells can then be hung from the net for luck.
- Taking a favourite toy or something which belongs to, or smells of, the caring adult to sleep with can act as a transitional object to help the child across the separation gap.
- Drawing a picture of the fear is sometimes helpful, using thought bubbles if needed. This helps to externalise the fear.

THE TWO PRINCESSES AND THE WALLED CASTLE

Lori   Age 8y

Past sexual abuse

Eight weekly sessions and ongoing support

The background

Lori was referred by her teacher who was concerned about her behaviour in class and with her peers. Eight years old, she was a very bright girl and in some ways ahead of her classmates. However, she would only work when she wanted to and was continually in some sort of dispute with others who claimed that she was spiteful and mean. She was also very moody and could be generally disruptive if not given constant attention. Her mother had also complained about her behaviour at home which, although never good, had become much worse since the mother had acquired a new partner.

In an interview with Lori's mother, she explained how Lori had been abused as a very young child by her own father. The mother felt that the abuse, although not severe and only on one occasion, was still the primary cause of Lori's unsettled behaviour. Lori had been offered therapy but had refused to continue the sessions. During bouts of bad behaviour at home and when she was not getting her own way she accused her mother of not protecting her from her father. These accusations were doubly upsetting to Lori's mother since she herself had been abused as a child by her own father.

Lori had two younger half-brothers, who, although difficult, did not display the same bursts of anger and resentment as Lori. In addition, they appeared to have a much better relationship with the mother's new partner. Lori, on the other hand, and according to her mother, went out of her way to be as difficult as possible. She had behaved in a similar fashion towards her mother's previous partner, the father of her two half-brothers.

It was difficult for Lori to trust anyone especially since, in her own words, people were always asking her questions about what had happened and she didn't want to think about it. From the beginning, it was made plain that things would progress as fast or as slowly as Lori wished. The play was as non-directive as possible.

Lori began by telling stories which explored her relationship with her mother. Any men in her stories were invariably bad. For further assessment purposes Lori attended the next few sessions with her best friend. In play Lori appeared manipulative and domineering, using sabotage when she did not get her own way. It became apparent that she had adopted the tyrannical victim role.

To Lori all men were bad, but she had a vested interest in them remaining so for in that way she gained the attention she craved. It was decided to confront the problem in various ways. The Behavioural Support team were called in to work with Lori on her social behaviour, looking at models of social behaviour and setting boundaries. Pacts were made at home to improve the relationship between Lori and her stepfather and I continued to work with Lori on male role models.

After several sessions Lori and I returned to the non-directive story telling and enactment. Her stories were less frenetic, more peaceful. One of her favourite themes concerned a princess who lived in a walled castle. Lori decorated the room and took a long time dressing herself up as the princess. She then proceeded to explain how the castle had huge thick walls and no one could ever get into it. The princess herself never went out.

After playing through being the princess on various occasions Lori asked if her best friend could come again for a session. This time Lori listened to her friend, let her choose some material and accepted some of her ideas on dressing up. It was obvious, however, that Lori very much wanted to continue the theme of the princesses in the walled castle. They took turns in telling the story of the two princesses. This is the story Lori told.

Once upon a time there were two princesses. They were best friends and they lived in a huge castle in a far away land. The castle was really big and it had very, very thick walls. It also had another thick wall which went all the way round the outside. No one could ever get into the castle and the two princesses never went out. Inside the castle it was very beautiful because the two princesses had spent a lot of time decorating it. The princesses were very beautiful too and they both had long blonde hair. They wore long dresses down to their ankles, one wore bright blue and one wore bright pink. They also had head-dresses, sort of scarf things over their hair. They played games every day and were very happy looking at themselves in the mirror.

One day while the princesses were playing a bad man got into their castle. He climbed up the plants which grew up the castle walls. The princesses didn't know he was there until he came right into their bedroom. They were very frightened, but they got hold of him and tied him up in some of the material they were playing with. Then they took him outside and threw him over the castle wall. They weren't sure that he was dead though, so they went outside and buried his body deep in the ground. The bad man never came back and the two princesses lived happily ever after.

The outcome

Lori had insisted on burying the body of the bad man under a pile of material. Before the burial, which took a long time, she had shown great delight in jumping up and down on the giant teddy bear which had played the part of the bad man. There was a great deal of emphasis placed on the fact that the bad man was dead and that he would not be able to come back.

With support, Lori had been able to go beyond the walls of her castle to confront her bad man, overcome him and make sure he never returned.

Things began gradually to improve for Lori from that time on. There were still incidences of spiteful and manipulative behaviour but Lori was much more able to listen to reason. She was much less angry. It seemed as if she felt less threatened, less retaliatory. The situation at home started to improve. Her stepfather had been making big efforts and Lori was beginning to accept his offers of reconciliation. Gradually the attention she craved came from her positive rather than negative behaviour. Some sessions later Lori said that she never even thought about her real father any more. Her mother said the subject had not been mentioned since.

N.B. No supporting exercises and activities have been included here since issues of sexual abuse should always be referred to specialists trained in this field.

THROUGH THE WALL

Diana   Age 13y

History of past abuse

Weekly sessions over four months

The background

Diana, aged 13, was initially referred because she was at grave risk of expulsion due to her inability to function within the school setting without resorting to such behaviour as temper tantrums, stealing and foul language. Not much information was given about her past life apart from that she was on the Child Protection Register and was not allowed to see her father. She was living at that time in a foster-home, having been through various other homes where the foster-parents had been unable to keep her, due to her behaviour. Her current foster-mother was an extremely experienced lady and it was thought that if she was unable to keep Diana then this was the end of the road for this form of care.

The previous sessions

At the very first meeting with Diana and the Deputy Head of the school, Diana displayed resentment and mistrust, avoiding eye contact and any physical touch whatsoever. It was obvious that the main issue would be to gain her trust if any progress at all were to be made.

In the very first session no attempt was made to engage directly with Diana but, following the ideas of the revolutionary horse-trainer Monty Roberts who applies the same methods in his work with troubled adolescents, I pretended to ignore Diana while sorting out some fragile glass animals, some of which were broken.

Diana became interested in spite of herself. I had collected these animals as a child and had not looked at them for a long time, and we almost seemed to be reversing roles as she began to try to stand up the broken animals while I exclaimed with genuine dismay over how many were broken. Thus the divide between the 'healer' and the 'patient' was somehow breached. She chattered on happily and we talked about anything. I asked questions if they appeared relevant, but no attempt was made to talk about why we were there. We then made models out of clay and Diana made a model of a baby dinosaur which she nicknamed Dibber, it having been her nickname as a child. She was fiercely protective of Dibber and said that she would bring him the following week so that we could make up some stories about him.

After the first session we parted as friends.

Over the next few weeks Diana grew less and less mistrustful, more open in talking about herself and her problems, and eye contact became less of a problem for her. The methods used initially involved art and clay work when we created fantasy worlds and animals through which Diana could explore herself and her wishes within the safety of pretence. This gave Diana the chance to find out what she was good at and what she *did* have which was good in her life which obviously raised her self-esteem and overall level of happiness.

Some weeks into the sessions Diana began to display some anger. We worked with this by building anger mountains, using the corners of the room as 'feeling' faces (see p. 71) and making masks. One week she was not allowed to come to the session as she had to make a cake in a cookery exam and during the following week she went into the space where we worked and 'trashed' the cupboard. (A not uncommon reaction when therapy is stopped prematurely for any reason.)

The following session Diana and I drew out her cake. Into it we put the ingredients that we felt would make a successful contract or 'cake' such as commitment and trust in the place of flour and eggs. When it came to how long the cake needed for baking Diana was reluctant to stipulate a time, so I explained that it just meant that after, say, four weeks we could take the 'cake' out of the oven to see if it was done. If it needed longer the timer could be reset.

Diana seemed happy with this arrangement and added a further ingredient: 'effort'. When I asked what she meant she said 'Well, you know, behaviour and stuff.'

We came then to the 'performing' stage of the sessions (see Chapter 8, 'Group Work'). Some psychodramatic techniques, together with a form of playback theatre, where events in an individual's life are 'played back' or acted out were used. In this way, we invented a character who, to all intents and purposes, was Diana herself. Through the safety of this character Diana was able to review, from her now more mature position, the bad experiences of her earlier years. She was also able to acknowledge and assimilate anything she was ready to take on. She showed great enthusiasm for this work painstakingly creating the story which neither of us ever acknowledged was hers. Only once did she say, looking at me with an arch expression on her face 'It's a bit like me, ain't it Miss?'.

Over six weeks we played 'Sara's' story through creating scenes and taking it in turns to play various parts. As the weeks progressed, Diana often wanted to play the whole story through from the beginning again until finally in week six, she announced that she had had enough. The story was finished; could she please have a copy of it?

After the half-term holiday there was a change in Diana. She had been having fewer instances of bad behaviour and her teachers were cautiously pronouncing themselves pleased with her progress. She appeared calmer and more in control. We talked a little about the future, and she said that one day she would like to have a car. She said she would like to make up a story about herself and her car. The following is her story.

Once upon a time there was a girl who had a new car. She drove everywhere in it but there was one place she really wanted to go. It was a very special, beautiful place but she couldn't get there because it was blocked by a very big wall. The wall was huge but because it wasn't as beautiful as the place behind it, it covered itself in big black, thorns.

The girl really wanted to go to the beautiful place so she asked for some help and with a friend she drove the car at the wall and made a huge hole in it. She went through the hole into the beautiful place and really enjoyed it, but she wanted to go back and knock every bit of the wall down before she could stay there. Her friend got out of the car and she knocked the rest of the wall down herself.

The girl and her friend agreed that they could get into the beautiful place any time they wanted to now, but the girl said that it wouldn't do to let everyone in, only certain people.

Later, the girl seemed a bit sad and said that beautiful places didn't really exist. Then she said that maybe they did but not for long. She agreed with her friend that it was good to let people see the beautiful places whilst they were there.

The outcome

We acted through this story, building the wall out of chairs. When it came to knocking down the wall Diana 'drove' at it with such enthusiasm that the chairs went flying everywhere. It seemed that in more ways than one, she had made a 'breakthrough'.

Over the last three sessions we acted through the fairy tale of 'Ricky of the Tuft' looking at different attributes. Diana enjoyed being the magic fairy and loved the empowerment of granting the gifts – that the ugly babies would have wit and humour but that the beautiful one would be stupid. She went away thoughtful after the penultimate session having decided that she would rather be ugly and witty than beautiful and dumb and saying 'I guess no one really has it all.'

The ending of our sessions after nearly five months of work was very important. Diana had agreed that the 'cake' was cooked and going back into lessons meant that she could take part in a drama production for the end of term. She felt she was an expert at drama now!

Diana drew her lifeline in brilliant colours. It was surrounded by black and with blood red which she said represented the tears which came from her being hit around. Schools were represented by suns peeping from behind the black and green – the escape into the hills. The future was yellow with other vibrant colours in a long line representing travel and a baby, remaining in school and in her foster-home. We agreed that some black was necessary for without it the other colours wouldn't show up as much. There were other children there too in Diana's picture, children she would one day foster herself.

Diana remained at her foster home and at school she gained her five GCSEs. The last I heard of her was that she was in a stable relationship with a baby of her own.

Supporting exercises and activities

The sideways approach

Especially with adolescents and with children who have had an amount of previous intervention, there is often a degree of mistrust – a kind of 'oh no, here we go again' attitude. The approach adopted by Monty Roberts in his training of difficult horses and work with children is to pretend to be completely disinterested in them, allowing the horse, or child to come to him, in effect starting where they are – at their level. With difficult children the trick is therefore, to take out something that you know they will find interesting, and then proceed not to show it to them. When they do become interested, treat their interest as nothing unusual but continue to be occupied yourself, answering any questions but letting the moves come from them.

Drawing up contracts

With children for whom trust is a major issue, some sort of contract is advisable even if this is over a short time. The metaphor of a cake appeals especially to younger children and they can be encouraged to add whatever ingredients they feel will help the cake to cook properly. The idea of the 'timer' can also be used to establish how long the child can hope to have the attention. The mixing bowl and its ingredients can be drawn as can the final cake when it comes out of the oven. The act of putting this down on paper establishes the concept more firmly.

Dealing with feelings

- Recognising and externalising feelings helps us to deal with them. Drawing out, embodying and sculpting can help with this.
- Draw 'feeling' faces, such as sad, happy, angry or afraid ones, on large pieces of paper and place them in different parts of the room.
- Encourage the child to stand in the different places and act as if he has the corresponding feeling. See how easy it is for him to do this with certain feelings.
- Ask the child what he does when he has this feeling.
- Ask the child how he would know if someone was feeling like this, how it would show on their body etc.
- Encourage the child to embody the feeling.
- Talk about how sometimes you can have more than one feeling at the same time. Embody both or all feelings, going from one to the other.

Playback theatre

This technique involves telling your own story to a group of actors and then watching them act it through, thereby portraying a situation in a different light. It is not advised that this technique be used without previous training.

Chapter 5

The Use of Pre-written Material and Recurrent Themes

As they went out into the sunshine all memory of the Snow Queen's palace and its empty splendour vanished. There they sat, the two of them, and it was summer, a beautiful summer's day. ('The Snow Queen', *The Walker Book of Fairytales*, A. Ehrlich)

Fairy tales, myths and legends

Fairy tales give children hope. Although most of my work centres around the telling by the child of his own story, there are occasions when a particular fairy tale or myth, carefully chosen, read or told and acted out has allowed the child to project his own hopes and fears onto the characters and themes of the story thus concretising them and giving him a belief in the inevitable power of good over evil. The stories the children tell themselves are often mythical or fairy-tale-like in character, reflecting as they do their themes of good versus evil, struggle, transformation and magic.

Left to themselves, children often experience fears which may seem formless. Being able to project these fears onto the characters and events in fairy tales gives them a name and helps to give the child something that he can come to grips with. It is easier to struggle with a wolf than with an insubstantial black shadow.

Without fairy tales the world would be full of formless, shapeless dark shadows. With fairy tales the child can come to grips with his own anxieties. He can encounter his deepest fear and his most fervent hope in story form, thus distancing himself and beginning to look at himself more objectively.

Fairy tales offer a child an assurance that there is always a compensatory factor. In this they align with Jung's view of the psyche's struggle towards 'Wholeness' and the compensatory functions of the subconscious, as in dreaming (see Chapter 3, 'The Significance of Metaphor and Symbol in Dramatherapy'). For every wicked witch there is a good fairy; for every kindness, a reward; and for every injustice, a fitting retribution. A character may be puny, as in 'Little Thumb', but he has a wise head on his shoulders.

From time immemorial stories have been told, handed down by word of mouth before they were written. What is astonishing is not that there have been so many stories but that the themes that they express, even in stories told in places and times as far flung as ninth-century China, 17th-century France or 21st-century England should be so similar.

Archetypes

One possible reason for this is that fairy tales, myths and legends hold archetypal content. Archetypes, according to Jung, are highly charged energy patterns of the collective unconscious. They are aspects of our psyche which resonate with certain figures or themes in the universal unconscious. They do not belong to this or that person but rather to the trend towards certain types of symbolic representations inherent in all of us. Thus we may all at times play out the brave warrior, or childlike princess, the clever magician or wicked witch.

At the same time as being representative of the archetypal powers within each of us, fairy tales contain a belief in the victory of the good forces over the evil. For example, kindness will be rewarded with wealth and a good marriage, and wickedness with destruction. This belief, it may be argued, is part of what makes fairy tales so suitable for use with children whose backgrounds often seem to offer little hope. The outcome may remain the same, but to carry on without hope makes the world a much darker place.

Recurrent themes

This struggle between good versus evil and the eventual victory of the good forces is a central theme in most fairy tales although not necessarily in myths and legends. With older children and especially in group work, myths, representing as they do the symbolic journey or quest towards the Whole, may be useful in providing the children with opportunities to explore their own stages of development and the often complex feelings initiated by life's vagaries. The myth of Theseus and the Minotaur for example (see Chapter 8, 'Group Work') allows children not only to enter into the labyrinth of chaos and uncertainty, a true representation of adolescence, but also offers them the chance to reflect on such human attributes as courage, bravery and trust, as well as the human frailties of arrogance, disloyalty and betrayal.

Another theme found in numerous early fairy tales, myths and legends is that of the long, protracted sleep during which time the world is being made ready to receive the coming of the new hero. It happens to Snow White and Sleeping Beauty as they await the arrival of their prince, to King Arthur who sleeps still, waiting for his country's call, and again the Volsung Saga as Brynhild waits to be awakened by Sigurd. If something is worth having, it is worth waiting for might seem to be one message that can be derived from these tales, which is the opposite of the modern-day trend of 'have today, pay tomorrow'.

Themes such as abandoning children in times of famine, laying a trail as guidance and ogreish cannibalism are found separately or combined in stories in languages as far flung as Zulu and Greek. 'Babes in the Wood' and 'Little Thumb' contain all three themes while the Russian tale 'Vasilisa the Wise' follows a similar trend of poverty, abandonment or exclusion, cannibalism and magical guidance. For children for whom neglect is a part of their lives, being brave enough to use their own initiative, proving that they can manage alone and being rewarded for it by magical intervention or a fortunate turn of events, is an empowerment which acting through stories with this theme can give them (see the following case study).

Other common themes include that of the youngest child, who is often the hero in fairy tales and who is always good and kind even in the face of extreme provocation, who is persecuted but whose goodness is rewarded by supernatural intercession. 'Cinderella' is perhaps the most famous of these stories but 'Snow White and the Seven Dwarfs' and 'Toads and Diamonds' as well as 'Vasilisa the Wise' follow a similar thread. In true fairy-tale tradition these stories speak of the strengthening of self before magical help intervenes.

Sometimes this strengthening of self involves a realisation which is transformative. A common theme is the realisation of the power of love, often symbolised by a kiss. Here again fairy tales offer hope. Those who are ugly or deformed or even stupid by accident of birth may be transformed by love as in 'Ricky of the Tuft' or 'Beauty and the Beast'.

Men released from bestial spells by the attentions of lovely young women figure largely in fairy tales. The proverbial toad – a being of the lowest vibrational order, from the realms of the subconscious is changed by a kiss into a Prince – a glittering figure, almost more than human – the epitome of higher consciousness. This theme may well owe its origins to the myth of Cupid and Psyche as written by Apuleius in *The Golden Ass*.

The sting in the tale

Much has been written about the morality of fairy tales, and it is not my intention to go deeply into that here. Suffice it to say that every ancient story has its point, its reason for having been told in the first place. Myths are often more transparent since they are, according to Ernst Pederson, a chaplain in a psychiatric hospital who has done much work with fairy tales, 'a symbolic expression capable of "verbalising" an internal experience which otherwise cannot be easily formulated' (Brun *et al.* 1993: 79).

Fairy tales also deal with the idea of symbolic journeys of the self. Little Red Riding Hood must leave the comfort of her childhood home to struggle through the dark forest of her subconscious and grapple with her deepest fear in the form of the wolf. Cinderella must know what it is like to be completely alone and yet not give in to despair before the fairy being, her higher consciousness, arrives with her magical transformative powers.

Also inherent in fairy tales is the principle that it is not the outward appearance which is important but the inner essence, even though this is sometimes disguised and may need help to come to revelation. Thus we have extremely small men performing impossibly great feats as in 'Little Thumb' or extremely ugly looks which hide beautiful beings and which need only the passage of time and strength in times of adversity to come to realisation as in 'The Ugly Duckling'.

It is part of the attraction of fairy tales to the child that in them anything is possible. At a time when all seems impossible, when the hero or heroine has given every last ounce of his or her strength or resolve, that is when the magic happens, the transformation occurs, the fairy arrives, the kiss transfigures. Birgitte Brun, in her book *Symbols of the Soul* explains that 'The fairytale does not tell us about a happy solution being reached without any effort.' This means that 'the child does not come through its crisis until it is ready to develop through struggle' (Brun *et al.* 1993: 51). Fairy tales, myths and legends tell us that it is part of our development to make mistakes: that it is often a healthy thing to do and that we need to make many mistakes before we reach our goal. The point is not to give up.

Thus it may be said that fairy tales speak to the child about what is important to him: about what and who he is going to become, about the struggles that he is going to have in reaching that goal, about the lessons he must learn and the surprises, good and bad, that may be waiting for him along the way. They speak to him about his relationships with others and with the supernatural, of that belief in magic which as an adult, one day, he may lose. They offer him assurance of the power of good over evil and show him that it is in his best interests to be good. They contain his fears and most importantly give him hope for the future.

Case study

BABES IN THE WOOD

Andy and Jed   Age 7y and 8y

Severe sibling rivalry

Ongoing weekly sessions

The background

Jed and Andy were referred to me by the SENCO following concerns about their behaviour separately in class and together in the playground. One of the major worries was the fact that the two boys seemed to hate each other. They were always picking fights with each other and this would almost always end in tears usually with one of them being hurt. Jed and Andy were half-brothers. Neither of them knew their fathers, and their mother, who also had another younger child, was expecting her fourth baby by another man who had already disappeared from the family. The children frequently came to school hungry and poorly clothed although they showed no signs of any physical abuse.

In the first session their dislike and jealousy of one another was obvious. They were unable to share or take turns at anything. I decided to give them separate sessions to let them each find their own way into this method of working. The younger lad, Andy, was very imaginative and was soon making up and acting out his own stories with the use of the material. The older boy, Jed, was quieter and more thoughtful, preferring to talk and saying that he couldn't make up stories. I allowed him to talk and play the story-bag game, encouraging him to act out, if only in part, any story he gave me.

Finally I judged that it was time for them to share sessions and watch each other's work. At first it was very hard work insisting on each watching and valuing each other's stories. However, each week it became slightly easier and they were able to sit and appreciate each other for increasingly longer periods of time. Once they realised that they each had an equal amount of time and attention their demands grew fewer. One day they asked if they could do a story together. I agreed.

It was a disaster. They were unable to agree on anything and it seemed as if we were back at square one. I decided they were not yet at a stage where they could accept each other's ideas enough to act upon them and that they would therefore need ideas from me.

An obvious choice of story was 'Babes in the Wood'. I told the story. They loved it immediately and proceeded to act it out with me playing the roles of the bad stepmother, the father and the evil witch.

They dressed up and decorated the Rainbow Room with material, creating a forest and the old witch's house with its fire. The following is their version of the story.

Once upon a time there was a man who was a woodcutter. He lived on the edge of the forest with his two boys and his new wife. His first wife, the boys' mother, had died. His new wife was horrible to the boys and never fed them even when there was food. One day she told her husband that there was no food left and that he would have to take the boys to the forest and kill them. The more the boys pleaded, the more their mother told them to go.

Their poor father took the boys to the deep forest and took out his knife. The boys pleaded with him and said that they would disappear, get out of his way, and no one would ever know. The father

couldn't kill them and so he told them to stay in the forest and look after themselves as best they could. The boys spent the night under a tree, huddled together, very cold and hungry. But the youngest boy had been very clever, he had left a trail of little pebbles behind as their father led them into the forest, and the boys now followed this trail back home.

Their father was pleased to see them, but his wife was furious. She demanded that the boys be taken into the forest again. This time the eldest boy left a trail of crumbs, thinking that they could follow these home. But the next day, when the boys went to follow the trail, they found that the birds had eaten all the crumbs. They were alone and lost in a big dark forest.

They wandered around for a long time not knowing what to do until they found a lovely little house which was made of sweets and tasty things to eat. They were so hungry that they began to break bits off. Suddenly a loud voice frightened them and a horrible-looking witch with a black cloak and long pointed nose waved her broomstick at them. Instead of frightening them away though she gave them a big meal...and another...and another. The boys grew fatter and fatter. They wondered why the witch was being so nice to them when really they knew she was a horrible person.

One day they found out. The witch had got up early to put lots of wood on her fire. She asked the youngest boy to help her. While he was there she caught hold of him and tried to put him on the fire to cook. The eldest boy saw what was happening and ran to rescue his brother. Then they both turned and threw the old witch on the fire where she crackled and spat.

The boys then went home to their father who was so pleased to see them. The bad stepmother had mysteriously disappeared at the same time as the witch. The three of them – the boys and their father – lived happily ever after.

The outcome

Both boys loved acting out this story. They took it in turns to be the one doing the rescuing and they devised new and different ways to trick the witch into stepping into the fire. Each time they acted it out they grew physically closer, as when they huddled in the forest, and spoke more in unison, as they stood up to their stepmother and the witch.

After some weeks teachers began to remark that the fighting had grown less and that the boys had even been seen sharing conkers.

Both boys still attend the occasional session as part of ongoing support. They are able to create and act out stories together with very little disagreement. Hardly one session passes without them asking to do 'that one about the witch'.

Supporting exercises and activities

Stories hold different meanings for different people. What one child will take from one story may be different to another child. For this reason it is advised when using pre-written material such as fairy tales, myths or legends to allow the child to draw his own conclusions. A general discussion about the story may be useful, but in no way should allusion ever be made as to similar events or characters in the child's own life. By leaving the story in the land of metaphor, as explained in Chapter 3, a safe framework for exploring the content is created.

Some suggestions for stories which I have found useful are as follows:

- 'Dick Whittington' for dealing with moral dilemmas;
- 'Babes in the Wood' for dealing with issues of neglect and sibling rivalry;

- 'The Ugly Duckling' for dealing with low self-esteem;
- 'Little Red Riding Hood' for dealing with fears about being lost and fear in general;
- 'The Three Little Pigs' for encouraging working together;
- 'Cinderella' for dealing with family issues;
- 'Sleeping Beauty' for issues about loyalty and broken promises;
- 'The Snow Queen' for encouraging perseverance;
- 'Aladdin' for extending imagination;
- 'Tom Thumb' and 'Ricky of the Tuft' for dealing with issues about personal values;
- the myth of Theseus and the Minotaur for issues surrounding loyalty and betrayal;
- 'The Sword in the Stone' to inspire empowerment;
- 'Vasilisa the Wise' for encouraging intuition;
- the myths of the Australian Aborigines' Dreamtime for exploring creativity;
- the Persian creation myth 'Ahura Mazda and Ahriman' for exploring the conflict of good versus evil.

Suggested sources for fairy tales, myths and legends are to be found in Appendix B (p. 105).

Summary

- Fairy tales give children hope in the power of good over evil.

- Fairy tales allow children to come to grips with their anxieties by giving form and name to their fears.

- The more concrete a fear, the easier it is to deal with.

- Fairy tales offer a belief in the existence of a compensatory factor.

- Archetypal content may be an explanation for the universality of fairy tales, myths and legends.

- Fairy tales have universal themes which are archetypal in content and may speak to us on deep levels.

- Myths represent the individual's symbolic journey towards 'Wholeness'.

- Fairy tales are a framework for exploring life, its struggles and successes.

- Fairy tales contain our fears and offer us hope.

Chapter 6

Dream Work

'Oh, I've had such a curious dream,' said Alice. (Alice in Wonderland,
Lewis Carroll)

Why do we dream?

As my work deals primarily with children's emotions it follows that my concerns are with anything which may affect these emotions. Dreams and, in particular, nightmares often have a role to play here. Many a child has come to me complaining that they have had the same nightmare on more than one occasion. Sometimes it is so bad that they are afraid to go to sleep. As with the occurrence of voices, we take the line that the dreams are trying to tell us something: that the mind is trying to sort out information in its own way. I often try to explain this to a child by using the analogy of a big chest of drawers. Everything has been tipped out onto the carpet during the day and now, at night, the mind is trying to sort it all back into the right drawers. Sometimes, when it has finished, there is something left which does not seem to belong in any drawer. This is the dream. Sometimes it has been left out because it needs to be noticed, and then we can find the right drawer to put it in.

As far as interpretation goes, it is vitally important that no outside adult analysis of children's dreams be attempted. Children's dreams are about children's issues. As has previously been explained we all have our own dictionary of symbols, and this is nowhere so true as in dreaming. The mind will present images which mean something only to us although we frequently do not understand them. During our waking moments we are constantly unconsciously assimilating sensations. These are locked into our mind and are released in a general stream-of-consciousness scenario when we sleep. In dreamtime our mind will freely associate, using these sensations in a sometimes amusing way – often through a play on words. Thus if we have felt stifled in a situation, we may dream that we literally can't breathe or that someone is suffocating us. If we have been presented with a problem or an idea which has been too big to digest, we may dream that we are being forced to eat a huge meal which we can't swallow. A friend of mine whose sister had just let her down badly dreamt that she, with others, was jumping from one skyscraper roof to the other and that her sister was helping people across. When it came to her turn, her sister held out her hand and then let her fall, literally letting her down.

It is therefore obvious that the only person who is able to decipher the true meaning of a dream is the dreamer since only he or she is aware of how the dream made them feel and what other situation in life makes them feel this way. This has to be very sensitively approached with children, as a child will assume that any interpretation by the adult is the 'truth'. Although a dream can be drawn or painted out it is not recommended that any dramatherapeutic method be employed in dealing with the dream without previous training.

In the case study on p. 83 and in the two stories which deal with dreams (on pp. 63 and 51), techniques from dramatherapy and from psychodrama were used to help the child understand the meaning of the nightmare. In every case, the child was given the control, something which he did not feel he had during the dream nor, probably, during the real-life situation. The enactment proceeded at the child's pace and in the child's time. No attempt has been made to analyse particular aspects of the dream and in some cases the reference to the real-life situation is purposely left oblique. The decision as to whether the dream, as the personal story, can be related to reality or is best left in the land of metaphor and symbol is down to the skill and experience of the dramatherapist and will depend on the individual child and particular case.

History of dreaming

Throughout the ages many cultures have believed that dreams are important communications sent by an outside source to warn us of danger or convey messages of hope. In particular the Egyptians paid great attention to the meaning of dreams and present-day dream study owes much to their investigations. The Greeks even went as far as to build shrines that served as dream oracles, where the dreamer would seek enlightenment on his waking problems through his sleep. In Australia the Aboriginal peoples believed that their world was fashioned out of the Dreamtime and children learnt of the importance of this level of consciousness from a very young age.

Modern-day Western medical thinking on the subject of dreams has its roots in the theories of Freud and Jung. Sigmund Freud (1856–1939) placed dreams firmly in the unconscious which he said was the home of repressed instincts and desires, and Carl Gustav Jung (1875–1961) gave us further levels of meaning with his conjectures about archetypes and the collective unconscious.

Nowadays we pay little or no attention to our dreams. Many people would go so far as to say that they never dream. Research tells us that we probably do all have dreams but we do not necessarily remember them. I have found dreams to be an invaluable source of information in helping me assess what is troubling a child. I now believe that children dream much more frequently than we realise and that their dreams are an important part of their psychological development.

Levels of meaning

Much has been written about dream analysis and psychoanalytical interpretation. The following is intended only as a rough guide to ideas which I have found useful in my work.

The theories of Freud and Jung suggested that the human mind operates on four levels:

1 the conscious mind, which is ruled by the ego;
2 the preconscious, where facts, figures and ideas are stored;
3 the personal unconscious, which holds half-forgotten memories, sensations and repressed emotions and desires;
4 the collective unconscious, which goes beyond the personal to house the deeper memories of the human race.

From this framework three main classes of dreaming may be deduced.

- Level 1 deals with material in the preconscious. Dreams that come from this class concern places, events and characters which exist in the dreamer's life. They can often be taken at face value although sometimes they are used symbolically.
- Level 2 is primarily concerned with the personal unconscious and relies upon symbolic language. It may be said that both Jenny (in the following case study) and Christie, with her

dream of the nasty aliens, were dreaming on this level. For even though one dream dealt with human and the other with non-human characters, both girls had invented symbolic characters to represent their fear.

- Level 3 contains material which comes from the collective unconscious. It is possible that Sarah was dreaming on this level when she conjured up her stone of life.

These levels are obviously interchangeable and no one dream necessarily corresponds entirely to one level. Dreams may fly in and out of levels or remain completely on one.

Key elements in children's dreams

Children begin to dream at a very young age. There is some evidence to suggest that babies may even dream in the womb. Since most of early life is concerned with physical sensations, it is likely that the dreams of babies and very young children are sensory in nature. As impressions and sensations of the outside world filter into the young child's consciousness so their dreams change in nature to explore these. Most dreaming occurs in the REM (rapid eye movement) sleep stage and as babies spend nearly two-thirds of their lives in this stage, it is possible that they may have many dreams.

As a child grows up, the experiences and sensations of the outside world begin to impress themselves on his mind. A key element in children's dreams is fear. This fear may manifest itself in the form of human or non-human characters depending on the level of dreaming. Aggression also plays a large part in many children's dreams. Occasionally the child is the aggressor, but more often than not they are the victim.

Research has shown that the monsters in children's dreams may represent two different aspects of the fear in a child's life, one internal and one external. They may represent the actual cruelty of some adults or the difficulty the child may have in assimilating the kind, nurturing characteristics of a primary carer with the perforce stricter, more disciplinary traits. On the other hand, it has been suggested that the witches, vampires and bogymen may represent those wilder, as yet untamed aspects of the child himself which he has difficulty is reconciling with the outer world of restraint and socially acceptable behaviour.

Dreams and dramatherapy

Whatever they may represent, it is a fact that children can often be so distressed by their dreams that they are unable to return to sleep or even sometimes to their own bed. Occasionally, it is the dream itself which is to blame for the child's disturbed emotions and behaviour during the day, as it was with Christie and Jenny, and sometimes, as with Sarah and the stone of life, the dream is a revealing part of a bigger picture.

In either case dramatherapy is ideally suited as the medium for laying the dream to rest and helping to restore the emotional balance for the child since both dreams and dramatherapy hold dramatic form. Dreams speak to us primarily through action, through visual image. Occasionally they have verbal content and there are some schools of thought which say that if a dream speaks to the dreamer in words which are remembered then these words are of vital importance.

However, whether or not a dream has verbal content, there are other elements to be found which are akin to drama such as setting, plot, characters and interaction between those characters. A dramatherapist may help to externalise those internal stories for the child by giving him a safe stage on which to play them out. The nebulous quality of dreaming lends itself more to the creative, right-brained, spatially aware approach of acting than to the more analytical, language-based left-brained method of verbal explanation and discussion.

In setting the stage for the enactment of the dream, it is of extreme importance that the child leads the way. The dream can then be played through with the child as chief actor/director. Psychodramatic techniques such as changing roles in the dream and speaking as different characters or objects may be used for clarification, as in Christie's dream when I asked her to speak as one of the aliens.

Depending on the circumstances I sometimes ask the child how the dream has made him feel and if he remembers having felt this way at any other time. I would normally then ask the child how he would have liked the dream to have ended. We then play through this new ending as many times as the child wishes, in a 'reframing' exercise. As with all sessions, it is always important to leave sessions on dream work on a positive note, and this 'reframing' exercise is very useful here. N.B. Reframing is not a technique which should be attempted without the appropriate training.

Both Freud and Jung stressed the importance of dreams in understanding the mind. Freud called dreams the 'royal road to the unconscious' and Jung was led to conclude that dreams were the most easily obtainable source of the ways in which people use symbols to express themselves. As a dramatherapist, I have found exploring children's dreams to be one of the most rewarding aspects of my work. There has always seemed to be three participants involved in these dream-work sessions: the child, myself and the dream. Once the dream has been noticed through enactment, it is as if something magical happens, it no longer holds any energy and fades into insignificance.

Perhaps, like the child, it needed only to be valued.

Case study

THE SCARY MAN

Jenny   Age 9y

Four weekly sessions and ongoing support

The background

Jenny is the eldest of a large family. At nine years old and with many younger brothers and sisters, she was already feeling a premature responsibility for life. She had originally been referred through her teacher at the request of her mother over a particular problem which was worked with and eventually resolved. The problem stemmed from an overwhelming anxiety to do the 'right' thing, to be the 'perfect' daughter, a syndrome which often seems to affect the eldest child in a family.

From time to time the problem reoccurred, but never again in such severity, and it was more easily dealt with each time. Jenny then began to refer herself whenever she had worries and wanted a five-minute chat. From the first sessions, it had been obvious that these 'worries' were largely due to her sensitive and caring nature and to her feeling that she was or could be somehow responsible for the situation. She worried about her mother and father, who she felt didn't always look after themselves properly. She worried about her little brother who wasn't sleeping very well, and even about the kitten that had once run out into the road and might do so again.

We worked together with Jenny's mum on allowing Jenny to play and make mistakes as any child would. Jenny's mum made some changes in the bedroom arrangements which gave Jenny less responsibility for her younger sisters and more room to play. Jenny's work at school improved and for a while she made no requests to see me.

Then, one day she arrived, very distressed, to say that for three nights running she had had nightmares and that now she was scared to go to sleep in case they came again. These were Jenny's dreams.

The first scary man

I was coming home from the shop. Mum had asked me to go and get a pint of milk. Suddenly a man appeared and started to chase me. I ran and ran. Then I turned round hoping he had gone but he hadn't. He was still there. So I ran again only my legs wouldn't move very fast. Then I turned round again and this time he was even closer. I ran again and every time I turned round he was even closer.

Then suddenly I was running towards the school and just as I got there he caught up with me and then I woke up.

The second scary man

I was in our caravan with my family on holiday. I was on my own in the caravan – all the others had gone somewhere. Suddenly I saw a man looking at me through the window. He was standing very close to the caravan and I knew he was going to do something horrible. Then he caught hold of the caravan and started shaking it. It was rocking from side to side and I couldn't stand up.

It got closer and closer to the edge and then it started to roll. I think it crashed but I woke up.

How the dreams were used

Being chased and not being able to move quickly enough is one of the most common anxiety dreams. There has been some recent research done which suggests that a mechanism in the brain is activated during this time which paralyses our muscles and prevents us from actually acting out these dreams and being thereby a danger both to ourselves and others. Paradoxically the dreams actually arise because of the inability to act out the feelings of anxiety.

Working on this assumption, that Jenny needed to act through her feelings of anxiety, we played through both dreams. In both cases, having acted out the dream several times and discussed the underlying feelings to which the dream gave rise we decided to change the ending. The following are Jenny's ideas for the different endings.

Dream 1

When I reached the school, the man caught up with me and tapped me on the shoulder. I turned round to face him even though I was very frightened. He said he had been looking for his cat and he thought I might know where she was. He said he hadn't meant to frighten me. I said it was all right, but I didn't know where his cat was. He said thank you and walked away.

Dream 2

When the caravan was shaking I began to feel a bit angry about why this man was shaking our caravan so I decided to go outside and talk to him. He said that he had been trying to stop the caravan from rolling down the hill and he said he was very sorry for having scared me. We made the caravan safe and then he walked away.

The outcome

Jenny was very pink and energised having acted through the dreams and their different endings. She said she felt a lot better and not as worried that the dreams might come back. A week later she said that they had not returned and they have not since.

Although the particular family situation which the dreams referred to was out of Jenny's control, what she did have some control over was her reaction to the situation. We had discussed how these situations were always best left to the adults concerned and how Jenny might not know the full story. In addition there might not be anything to worry about and she should discuss this particular worry with her mother or father. However, the anxiety had rooted itself in the subconscious and as such would not necessarily respond to cognitive reasoning. It therefore had to be met on its own ground, so to speak and dealt with in a psychodynamic way.

There will probably always be worries for Jenny. Personality traits plus early family conditioning and her place in the family have produced a susceptibility to anxiety. However, the more that Jenny can confront her fears head on, as she did in her dream endings, the more she will have confidence that she can overcome them.

Supporting exercises and activities

Enactment of dreams, especially nightmares, should not be undertaken unless a trained therapist is present for fear of retraumatisation.

The following ideas may be helpful:

- Obviously, being given the time and space to talk about the anxiety with a sympathetic adult is paramount and may in some cases be sufficient.
- Drawing a picture or a cartoon strip of the dream as it is and then drawing another picture/cartoon strip of how the child wishes the dream to end may help 'reframe' the nightmare.
- Dreamcatchers, to 'catch' bad dreams are available in some art and craft shops.
- Imagining a wall of light around the bed in which the child is protected is sometimes helpful.
- Ask the child to imagine themselves enclosed in a bubble of light. They can 'draw' it around themselves with a forefinger. Any attempt to penetrate it rebounds on the intruder.
- Reference to the Native American legend in which every child has the divine right to protection and is surrounded by a ring of cool blue flames which protect him has also been known to capture a child's imagination and make him feel safer.
- Drawing out the fear – in Jenny's case, a picture of the scary man – and tearing it up, burning or burying it can be effective.
- Telling the frightening object or person to 'Go Away!' in a very loud voice, thus confronting the fear has also been known to work.

Summary

- Any enactment of a child's dream must only be undertaken by a trained professional, taken at the child's pace and with the child in control.

- In dramatherapy the approach is taken that a dream has information to impart.

- An outside adult interpretation of children's dreams is not appropriate or safe.

- Dreams are often the result of the mind playing with sensory impressions expressed by words which are then translated into literal images.

- The dreamer himself is the only person who understands how the dream made him feel and how this might be connected to his waking life.

- Despite historical importance attached to dreaming, modern-day societies pay little attention to this expression of the unconscious.

- Modern-day dream-analysis bases much of its thinking on the theories of Freud and Jung.

- The three levels of dreaming are derived from the four stages of consciousness as described by Freud and Jung.

- Fear is a key element in children's dreams, representing internal and external experiences.

- Dreams can be ideally expressed through dramatherapy since they themselves hold dramatic form and speak through action and visual images.

- Techniques from psychodrama and a 'reframing exercise' can be used to help the child understand the dream.

- A study of a child's dream can be a valuable asset in understanding the unconscious hopes and fears which affect his emotional stability.

Chapter 7

Working with Loss and Bereavement

Perhaps there is more understanding and beauty in life when the glaring sunlight is softened by the pattern of shadows. (Dibs in Search of Self, Virginia Axline)

The following chapter is intended to be of help to anyone having to deal with a child who has suffered a loss or bereavement of someone they were close to. It is worth remembering that a child does not necessarily have to experience the death of a significant person to be suffering from the same stages of grief. Divorce, separation or other family reorganisation can produce similar feelings and behaviours in a child. The chapter will include a brief synopsis of the stages of grief as well as an introduction to the way children grieve depending on their age, some references to work done for a bereavement charity for children and their families, a case study and some ideas which are appropriate for use in the classroom.

The stages of grief

It may be helpful to understand the general stages of grief as relating to an older child or adult before examining the specific way that young children show their grief. Grief is personal and the way a person reacts to the death or loss of a loved one is dependant on a hugely variant number of factors. Grief can be short-lived or it can last a lifetime. In many cases, however, grief can take the form of clearly defined stages. As a general rule it is considered that if a person seems to be unable to move on from one of the early stages of grief then that grief may be seen as 'complicated' and additional professional help or support may be needed. In addition, the progress through the stages of grief may not be a linear one but may, rather, be through, as it were, a succession of culs-de-sac which are not necessarily taken in order and may need revisiting. It is worth noting here that children experience similar stages of grief to adults, albeit with some notable differences which will be discussed later.

The first stage of grief is usually shock and disbelief, which can take the form of physical pain or numbness. Initially the person may carry on as normal which may give the impression that they don't care or that they are 'coping remarkably well'. The child may complain of stomach pains or a bad headache, or there may be apathy, withdrawal or abnormal calmness. A very young child will experience the world as an unsafe place where the unimaginable has happened and might happen again, and will become anxious about being separated from other loved ones. They may develop insomnia or fear of the dark. Continual reassurance is needed and sometimes the reinforcing of firm boundaries to restore the child's confidence that the rest of his world is not going to disappear as well.

Denial is the second stage and often occurs within the first 14 days. During this stage the bereaved person will often behave as if the loved one is still there. They may keep saying that they have seen them in a crowd or on television, or they may continue to include them in arrangements. Hyperactivity is characteristic of this stage and reflects the need to avoid the reality of the loss.

The third stage comprises a mixture of emotions and revolves around the growing awareness that the person has gone. The feelings may be intense or even savage at times and a child may feel bewildered by them and their uncontrollableness. At these times he may use behaviour that is extreme in order to reflect the savagery of his emotions, as did Timothy when he became like a small hunted animal hiding under the desk (see following Case study).

The feelings may be one or all of the following: yearning or pining – a need to revisit or find a reason for the death; anger against anyone and everyone who was even remotely connected; depression – beginning to feel the emptiness – and, with it, lowered self-esteem. (The ability to cry in this stage is helpful.) Here food may be an issue with the bereaved person either eating to fill the emptiness or losing interest and appetite.

Guilt is another sometimes-overlooked emotion. Children are still very egocentric in nature and assume that the world revolves around them. Therefore they easily imagine that they are the cause of events which happen around them, be it their parents' divorce or separation, someone leaving the family home or someone's death. At this stage it is worth taking the time to impress upon the child that it is not his fault and that many children feel like this. A group discussion may be helpful here. A child I once visited through the Children's Bereavement Charity was convinced that her father had suffered a heart attack because she hadn't loved him enough and had not wanted to visit him because he was often cross. She thought his heart had known that she hadn't loved him enough and it had had an attack because of this. She concluded that his death was all her fault.

Anxiety is another common emotion which can sometimes develop into panic as the bereaved person begins to understand the full reality of the loss. Anxiety and panic about the changes which the loss will necessitate may even bring about thoughts of suicide.

Acceptance and moving on are the final stages of bereavement, and normally take place any time after the second year after the death. The person begins to accept the possibility of life without the loved one and to embrace the changes that life brings, by reinvesting their energy in new events, for example relationships, rather than directing their energy towards the past.

How children grieve

Not all children grieve in the same way. Their personality, religious beliefs or beliefs of their family or community, their previous experience of death as relating to a family pet or grandparent, their own and their family's emotional stability are all relevant here and will affect the extent and intensity of their grief. Indeed a child's grief is very seldom purely personal. Very often the way the parents grieve will be the way the child grieves. The fact that Timothy's father was not dealing with his loss meant that Timothy was having problems too (see following Case study). In my work with the Children's Bereavement Charity I have often come across parents who are concerned that their child is not grieving openly for the lost relative, while hiding their own grief lest it upset the child.

This belief that grief must be hidden from the child, and that because a child does not understand it follows that they do not grieve has been, mistakenly, prevalent until fairly recently. The deceased was often not spoken about in front of the children, and children were often not allowed to the funeral. In my work I have met cases where the child was only told that their father had 'gone away' and it was not until years later that they learnt that he had died. Research has shown that the consequences of withheld sorrow may have dire consequences. Alida Gersie in the Introduction to her book, *Storymaking in Bereavement*, writes 'In my work with adolescents who had attempted suicide, I noticed how their plea for help with issues of "life, death and mourning" had often been ignored. We silence grief at our peril' (1991: 20).

An amusing expression which sums up the commonality of the way children grieve is 'Children grieve in puddles'. This aptly describes the way that a child's emotional state and/or behaviour can be overwhelming one minute and completely normal the next. It can leave the unsuspecting adult confused and bewildered when their child is in a state of uncontrollable sobbing and then, remembering a favourite cartoon on television, skips off laughingly to watch it. While it can be both shocking and upsetting for the parent to see their child slip in and out of grief so quickly, for the child, not only is it a form of relief, but it is also completely normal.

Under two years of age, children react to the atmosphere around them, and the fact that they do not understand what has happened does not mean that they do not grieve. Young babies may show disruption in sleeping or eating patterns, may cry incessantly or may be very irritable. When they are mobile, a child under two may search for the missing person and think that they are hiding somewhere. They may in turn be withdrawn or apathetic or lose interest in their toys or food. As has already been said, firm and continual reassurances and boundary-setting will go a long way towards comforting a child.

Between the ages of two and five a child may show their grief by becoming irritable or clingy. They may have temper tantrums and want to destroy everything. Fear of abandonment is strong at this age and the fear that the remaining parent will leave needs to be addressed with repeated assurances and explanations. Here it is very important to tell the child the truth simply and honestly. Euphemisms such as 'Daddy's gone to sleep' or 'Mummy's gone on a long journey' will only make the child scared of going to sleep or travelling themselves or for the surviving relative to do so. In addition it is important to explain to the child that the deceased's body is not working any more and therefore they will feel no pain. This is the difference between sleep and death because in sleep the body is still working.

A child at this age cannot understand the permanence of death and may ask repeatedly when the loved person is coming back, much to the distress of the surviving relatives. The family's own spiritual beliefs will come into play here, but on the whole it is better to use plain facts repeating that the loved person has died and cannot come back to life. Nature may be helpful here, with an examination of a dead sparrow, worm or even leaf and a discussion of how things die and other things are born in a continual cycle of change.

By the age of eight a child usually has some conceptual comprehension and can understand the meaning of death. They may also start to be aware of the social impact of the death or loss and may start to feel responsible in some way. The issue of guilt has been dealt with earlier. At this age children like to believe that the world is an ordered place where there are routines and structures. Within this safe framework they are beginning to branch out to a world outside their family and explore relationships with their peers and at school. Experiencing a significant loss can throw them back into believing that the world is an unsafe place and they may exhibit regressive behaviour similar to that of the more emotionally volatile pre-school child. A return to temper tantrums is common, if very wearying, and, again, an emphasis on structure within the family and school environment can be helpful.

As a child grows older he becomes more aware of the finality of death, of its universality and inevitability. He also begins to recognise the possibility of his own death.

In adolescence the feelings and stages of grief approximate to adulthood except that they may be complicated by the teenager's rapid physical and emotional development.

Possible areas for concern

Just occasionally a child may adopt one or more of the following coping strategies which, if continued over a long period of time, may be unhelpful or even harmful.

If a parent has died a child may wish to find a substitute mother or father in the form of a teacher or friend of the family and this may give rise to complications and further loss scenarios.

The child may resort to aggressive behaviour in and out of school, may be frequently involved in fights or may become a school refuser. Anti-social behaviour such as drug abuse may arise here.

The child may adopt a strategy of helplessness and withdrawal, showing a lack of curiosity and engagement with life in general, even becoming deaf in extreme circumstances.

If the death or loss has been traumatic or the child has been involved in or witnessed disturbing scenes, Post-Traumatic Stress Disorder (PTSD) may be suspected if one or more of the following behaviours are noted.

- Frightened or highly disorganised behaviour which lasts for a long time.
- Repetitive play in which the themes or aspects of the death are expressed.
- Repetitive distressing dreams surrounding the event or frightening dreams without recognisable content.
- Repeated flashbacks, either audial or visual, of the event.

Professional help should be sought if any of the above occur.

Case study	
Timothy	Age 8y
Ten weekly sessions	

The background

Timothy was first referred by his teacher who was concerned over his frequent temper tantrums, behaviour which she said was almost psychotic in nature. After a display of extreme anger he would retreat under a desk where he would remain, head in hands, growling like a small hunted animal if anyone tried to entice him out. Timothy was the youngest in the family with an older very intelligent sister. His teacher said that he suffered from low self-esteem, always proclaiming that his work was 'rubbish'. Constant praise had some effect, but the temper tantrums were unpredictable and disturbing for other children in the class.

In an interview with Timothy's mother I learnt that although never an easy child Timothy had seemed reasonably stable until about eighteen months previously when her husband's brother had died in a particularly violent and unpleasant manner. The whole family had been seriously affected as they had been very close to him. Timothy had had a special rapport with him since everyone said that they were so much alike.

She said that her husband was not coping with the death at all well and refused to talk about it with anyone. In fact the deceased's name was hardly ever spoken.

I explained that I thought that Timothy could be helped by his father if his father could be persuaded to talk to Timothy about his feelings. I also explained that I felt that Timothy was dealing (or not dealing) with the death in the same way as his father. After some time and gentle encouragement by Timothy's mother, his father was persuaded to talk to Timothy about the death. The work I did with Timothy was taken home and the family began slowly to talk about their loss.

The programme of work with Timothy went as follows:

- We made a memory box out of an old shoebox, decorated it with cut-out pictures of things the uncle liked, for example flowers to represent the garden, the sea and so on. The memory box would contain all the other items.
- We drew pictures of the uncle with speech bubbles for phrases Timothy remembered him saying.
- We wrote a poem about him, describing all the uncle's characteristics that Timothy remembered.
- We wrote down on slips of paper all the things which made Timothy angry about the way his uncle had died and threw balls of clay at them.
- We collected up the clay, made a model of the uncle with it and painted it wearing his favourite clothes.
- We wrote a letter to the uncle expressing anything which Timothy would have liked to have said to him had he known he was going to die.
- We made a salt sculpture by colouring salt with chalk and layering the salt in a glass jar, each colour chosen to represent a different memory of the uncle.
- We put up a star on the ceiling to remember him.

As Timothy took each new item he had made home to his family he was able to talk about it with his father, and gradually the father was able to begin to express his own grief through a desire to help his child.

Although he still has the occasional temper tantrum, Timothy's behaviour is now much more reasonable. He is always at his happiest on a Monday when he reports that he and his father have been on a long cycle ride together over the weekend.

Supporting exercises and activities

The activities and exercises suggested here are aimed at achieving the following outcomes:

- Making the loss real for the child. Sometimes the loss is hidden and not discussed, and the child has the additional task of hiding his feelings as well as coping with them. Hence Timothy chose hiding under the table as his coping strategy.
- Identifying and expressing emotions – externalising the internal – helping the child identify any of the following: sadness, anger, guilt, anxiety, betrayal, rejection, helplessness, loneliness, panic, shame, depression, restlessness, weariness, emptiness, relief, gladness, freedom.
- Helping the child adjust to the changes. Loss of a loved one may mean new responsibilities, new roles, new practical arrangements or a new house, new school or even new family. The child can be helped by these changes being identified and discussed.
- Helping the child to move on, to let go of the attachment, to accept the loss and 'internalise the deceased' (as Angela did with her story of 'The Water Princess') and then to look to the future with new plans, projects to look forward to.

Simple ideas which may be adopted in the classroom or at home are as follows:

- Make a memory box and decorate it. Put in pictures, photographs or any special objects which remind us of the special person.
- Write a poem or letter to the special person thanking them for all the things/times/memories/ qualities they gave us.
- Have a class talk about the seasons – how things change and die so that new things can be born. Start with a big picture/collage of a tree and trace its changes throughout the seasons.
- Talk about people we miss and have a night sky with stars to represent each person who has gone. (Useful for separated families as well.)
- Write down on a piece of paper all the things which make us angry about the loss of the special person and place on a large mat.
- Take some clay and throw it at the paper (as hard as you like!). Then make something useful/special out of the clay.
- Use different coloured salt (coloured with large chalks) to represent the different qualities or memories (good and bad) of the special person.
- Write a message to the loved one and tie it to a gas-filled balloon. Release the balloon.
- Read/act out the story of 'The Snow Queen' as it begins in wintertime with the grief of Gerda and finishes in the summertime as the sun shines again.

Summary

- Stages of grief may apply whether a child has experienced bereavement or loss.

- A child that becomes 'stuck' in one of these stage may need professional help.

- Children experience similar stages of grief to adults with some notable differences.

- The stages of grief are shock and disbelief, denial, growing awareness and a mixture of emotions including anger, yearning and depression. The last stage is acceptance and moving on.

- The way a parent grieves will very often determine how a child grieves.

- Hidden grief may have potentially harmful results in later life.

- Children slip in and out of grief. They may be said to 'grieve in puddles'.

- Because a child is too young to understand does not necessarily mean they do not grieve.

- Clinginess and regressive behaviour in the form of temper tantrums is common in the young child.

- Simple honest language is best and euphemisms may give rise to confusion.

- Firm repeated assurances and explanations together with strong boundary-setting and routines will help convince the child that his world is safe again.

- Prolonged distress in the form of flashbacks, disturbing nightmares or repetitive behaviour may need professional help.

Chapter 8

Group Work

When is group work appropriate?

In my work with children with emotional and behavioural problems I have found that there are certain children for whom I have felt group work was not appropriate. These are children whose individual process is not yet at a stage where they can tolerate other negative behaviour patterns without either adopting or adversely reacting to them. I therefore considered that work on their own defence mechanisms was necessary for these children before they could either benefit from or in any way contribute to group work.

However for those children who have acquired a more established sense of self in relation to others group work is not only appropriate but desirable. We do not live in isolation in the world. Indeed our every thought, word and deed is, more often than not, coloured by the judgements and reactions of others. After a period of individual therapeutic intervention it is therefore a valuable exercise to 'test out' the changes that have hopefully been made by allowing the child space to interact with others. Lori, in playing out her story of 'The Two Princesses and the Walled Castle' showed that she had acquired a sufficient sense of self and knowledge of social behaviour through the programme of individual support to be able to interact with her best friend in a far less threatening and manipulative way than previously.

Group work can open out opportunities for a child to add to his experience of life either by rehearsing possible future scenarios or by lending new perspectives to past situations. In this way the child's emotional literacy and stability is increased which in turn raises his self-esteem and self-confidence. To be able to explore his reactions to an event or to his peers within a safely held environment gives the child confidence that he will be in control in future unpredictable situations, if not of the events themselves then at least of his own emotional reaction to them.

Working in a group also provides the opportunity for these emotional reactions to be normalised. In this way the child need not suffer the added burden of guilt or confusion over the way he feels about a situation or person. He may learn that it is natural sometimes to feel resentful towards his parent's new partner or that it is normal to feel that he is to blame if a parent leaves the family home. Shared emotions help the child to feel less lonely and may break through various misapprehensions. Through group work, Martin (in the following Case study) came to realise that his 'showing off' made him less, rather than more, popular. Moreover, group work provides the arena for the child's realisation, acceptance and resolve to be witnessed. The other members of the group as well as the dramatherapist act as the witnesses to the individual's process and add to the power of his inner development. (The role of the witness is discussed more fully in Chapter 4.)

Role playing in group work

Being with others necessitates the taking on of a role. The significance of the roles we play is discussed in Chapter 4, but it is worth reiterating here that one of the ways in which a healthy psyche manifests itself is through a comprehensive system of functional roles. Group work is a useful medium through which to explore the individual's role repertoire, validating our functional roles and highlighting those which we may have taken on inappropriately. Through group work an individual may arrive at a stage where he feels safe and secure enough within the group to let the other members see him as he really is. This acceptance by the group allows the individual to accept himself, and the necessity to adopt dysfunctional roles to cover up one's inadequacies is therefore diminished. Thus it was that Martin was able to admit that his character, Rodney the Clown, was secretly afraid of fire and that was why he made all his animals do the tricks. Although remaining within the safety of the metaphor, Martin was nevertheless able to recognise that he had to take the risk of appearing as himself in front of the crowd for them to accept him, and that his 'animals with their tricks' or in other words, his 'showing-off antics' were no longer suitable or appropriate.

Group work, therefore, promotes the extension of the individual's role repertoire, encouraging him to develop a range of roles which are appropriate to different situations and persuading him to eliminate those behaviours which are unhelpful.

Application of group work

In general, as far as working within the school environment is concerned, dramatherapy for groups may be said to be applicable in two different ways. Firstly, a group may be set up to explore a particular deep issue or issues which it is felt the children have in common and which is preventing them from benefiting from their education. These issues may be parental divorce or separation, bereavement, past abuse or presenting problems such as low self-esteem, lack of self-confidence or uncontrolled anger. To employ therapeutic techniques as opposed to cognitive methods in dealing with groups such as these would necessitate a prior training as a therapist and there is not room in this book to go into detail about this way of working.

However, with some training in pastoral and group work (see Appendix B), a member of staff may wish to set up a group which deals with more social problems such as social-skills training or bullying, and may wish to draw on some of the ideas explained in this chapter.

Setting up a group

Points for consideration:

- As with individual work the nature of the space provided is paramount. The children must feel safe and secure within an area of clear boundaries and free from interruption, an area which is also of adequate size to allow for movement.
- The size of the group is important. Groups of between six to ten seem to work best. In general the more volatile the children and the deeper the problems the smaller the group needs to be.
- The age range must reflect the aims and objectives of the group. For example, a group comprising children taken from one year group generally works best unless the intention is to set up a pseudo-mentoring system.
- The single- or mixed-sex criteria must, again, reflect the objectives of the group. A more important decisive factor might be the nature of the children's presenting behaviour. For

example, six children displaying aggressive behaviour and one withdrawn child would probably not be conducive to productive group work. In general the best working model seems to
be a group consisting of children who have similar coping strategies and defence mechanisms.

- The length of the session needs to be considered. In order to structure a session properly a
  session needs to be at least 45 minutes long. This means that to allow time for movement in
  between lessons the session may need to run over two blocks. Much longer than one and a
  half hours and the session can lose its impact.
- The number of sessions also needs to be taken into account. One-off sessions seldom seem
  to have much long-term effect. A suggested programme might be between eight and 12
  sessions depending on the issues, age and characters of the children involved.

Structure of a session

An excellent book which explains in detail how to structure group sessions is Sue Jennings'
Creative Drama in Group Work (see Appendix B). A brief outline of essential points follows here
and a suggested session plan is given at the end of the chapter.

- Sessions may be divided into three stages: opening or warm-up phase, main development
  stage and the closure, de-role and relaxation phase.
- The first session should include the drawing-up of a group contract in which the group looks
  at such issues as confidentiality, expectations, punctuality and hopes and fears.
- Games are ideal for use in the warm-up phase and may reflect the stage of the group, for
  example, introductory name games, trust games, games for focusing and concentration and
  team-building games. Books which give excellent examples of such games are *Gamesters'
  Handbook* and *Gamesters' Handbook Two* by Donna Brandes and Howard Phillips (see
  Appendix B).
- The main part of the session may include improvisation and role play, sculpting, mask work
  or another activity. Here again Sue Jennings' book *Creative Drama in Group Work* is helpful.
- The closure phase of the session should include a de-roling exercise if applicable (see Chapter
  4) and a game, or a relaxation phase. The game may be a summing-up of the session or an
  acknowledgement of the totality of the group. The relaxation may include a visualisation exercise. An example of a visualisation exercise suitable for use with children is given at the end
  of this chapter.

Life of a group

Any group which meets over a series of sessions will go through various stages of development
almost seeming to take on a life of its own. For those inexperienced in leading groups it is worth
mentioning here a few areas to be aware of. J. F. Benson's book *Working More Creatively with
Groups* is a useful aid to those wishing to know more about the process of the group (see
Appendix B). There are various models of the developmental patterns of a group, but the one
most generally referred to by dramatherapists (see Benson 1995: 79-82) is B. L. Tuckman's five-
stage scheme of

1 forming,
2 storming,
3 norming,

4 performing,
5 mourning.

Forming

In this stage the group is very reliant on the leader. Expectations are raised and need to be met. The group looks to the leader for control and guidance. Firm boundaries and a measured pace to the sessions will help establish feelings of safety within the group.

Storming

In this stage the group is beginning to flex its muscles and challenge the authority of the leader. This must not be construed as 'failure' on the part of the leader. Rather, the leader must gently and firmly re-establish the boundaries while allowing the group room to find its own pecking order. Anger and hostility is common here as is competition and rivalry between members.

Norming

After the storming stage the group will hopefully begin to establish its own norms. Some groups revisit the storming stage from time to time depending on their own needs and the expertise of the leader. Members begin to have more faith in the group itself and are more ready to share their experiences. This is the beginning of the working phase of the group.

Performing

This is the stage of blossoming. Creative energy is released and the group functions as a whole; the whole being more than a sum of its parts. Some groups never reach this stage, but it is a very rewarding phase for all concerned if it can be achieved. A feeling of safety is manifest in the group and members will generally share many personal experiences. Care must be taken to hold these experiences safely and to spend adequate time in the closure phase.

Mourning

As the end of the life of the group approaches, members will often adopt various strategies to cope with it. There may be denial that the group experience has meant anything; commitment may decline; there may be sadness and guilt or even anger. Care must be taken by the leader to synthesise the past experiences of the group members into their own individual future hopes and dreams. Acknowledgement of the good and bad is necessary.

Case study

THE SECRET OF RODNEY THE CLOWN

Martin   Age 11y

Low self-esteem

Eight weekly group sessions

The background

Martin was referred by his Head of Year following concerns over his behaviour both in and out of class. He appeared very aggressive with few social graces, answering back all the time. In class he acted as a catalyst to his peers continually 'winding them up' and generally antagonising them by his showing off. Out of class he forced himself on others, always endeavouring to be the centre of attention. When he did not get the attention he required he played the victim. It was obvious from the first that his history of confrontations stemmed from feelings of inadequacy. His mother had been suffering from depression since her marriage to Martin's father had broken up, and Martin, an only child, felt in some way responsible. There had also been some history of soiling.

The sessions

Martin joined a group of three other boys and two girls from his year. At first he appeared to be somewhat antagonistic and he used his showing-off tactics to the rest of the group boasting about the super holiday he was going to have. He identified with a character which he called Rodney the Clown and seemed to be a natural at the clown antics. During the following sessions he began to share his experiences of being an only child and the worry over his mother with the rest of the group. Through Rodney he began to turn his 'acting out' strategies into plain acting. As Rodney he informed the group that he loved the performing although he didn't like the practising. As the sessions developed, Martin seemed less and less inclined to seek negative attention. His presence in the group was quieter except when he was being Rodney. Then he claimed the positive attention of the group through his acting.

Towards the end of the sessions the group began to volunteer more. One of the girls felt threatened by this new trend towards self-revelation and left the group. The remaining girl who was very quiet left with her. From then on the group 'blossomed' with each of the remaining boys working through some important issues by way of the characters they had chosen. In the penultimate session they wrote and then performed, using the group, a 'secret' that their character was keeping. The following story is Rodney's secret.

Once upon a time there was a clown who lived in a circus. He performed all sorts of tricks but the tricks that were the audience's favourite were those which were done with fire. Now Rodney had a secret – he was very afraid of fire and that was why he always got all his animals to do his fire tricks for him. One day when he was just about to get his animals to do the fire tricks the crowd started shouting 'Rodney, Rodney' and Rodney knew that they wanted him to perform instead. There was a burning hoop of fire and Rodney was really scared as he looked at it. But the crowd kept on shouting 'Rodney, Rodney' and finally Rodney jumped. Afterwards Rodney felt really good about what he had done. He said that people would be nice to him now. They had always put him down in the past because he would never do the fire tricks. From then on the crowd loved Rodney and he didn't really need his animals any more.

The outcome

Martin began to settle into class. He made a few close friends, one from the group, and was not singled out as a troublemaker again. Although from time to time he still got into trouble his tutors said that he was 'much better'. His boastful, showing-off behaviour, which used to antagonise his peers so much was not so apparent. In time he blended into the background of his tutor group. He joined the drama group at school and had the leading part in one of the end-of-year productions – as a clown!

Summary

- There may be some children for whom individual work is necessary before they can contribute to and benefit from a group.

- Group work is a helpful way of 'testing out' the work done with an individual child.

- Group work is a way of exploring, within a safe environment, relationship issues which arise in real life.

- Working in a group also provides the opportunity to normalise feelings and emotional reactions.

- Through group work an individual can explore their own role repertoire, confirming those roles which are useful and dispensing with those which prove dysfunctional.

- Being accepted by a group helps the individual accept himself.

- The group scenario lends weight to the potentiality of inner development in that the individual's process is witnessed by the other members.

- Within a school environment dramatherapy groups may exist on two different levels – an in-depth therapy group led by a trained therapist which explores significant issues or a social-skills-based group which looks at relationships between children.

- Points to consider in setting up a group are space, size of group, age range, same or mixed sex, characters of children and length and number of sessions.

- The structure of a session is roughly based around warm-up, main development and closure stages.

- Most groups go through a developmental life of their own. A working model is that of five stages: forming, norming, storming, performing and mourning.

Sample outline of session plan for dramatherapy group work

Group: Eight 11-year-olds, four girls, four boys

Length of Session: One and a half hours

Objectives: To explore issues of bullying

Number of session: Fourth of eight sessions

Warm-up phase

Game 1: stop the group

Objectives: team-building, awareness of group space

Group to move around the room finding a space and walking into it. One person designated to stop the group. When this person stops and starts the whole group follows.

Variations: take it in turns to stop and start the group; turn it into a guessing game – someone has to guess who is stopping the group.

Game 2: counting up

Objectives: working as a group

Group stands in a circle and one person starts by saying 'one'. Another says 'two', another 'three' etc. The aim is to see how far the group can count up together without two people speaking at the same time. If this happens, the group returns to 'one'.

Main development phase

- The group brainstorms an issue, for example, bullying, writing associated words on a flipchart.
- Relevant words are chosen and the group embodies them by making a sculpture out of their bodies, for example to show what a victim may look like. Opposites can be used here too.
- The group divides into two and brainstorms situations when they have observed or been involved in bullying.
- Group A acts out one of these situations.
- Group B observes and, if they feel they could change the victim's reaction in any way, they shout 'stop' take the place of the victim and allow the scene to continue with the changes. This form of enactment is called 'spectacting' as the spectators also participate as actors.
- Group B has a turn to act while Group A watches.
- A discussion follows on the scenes observed, the changes made and the group's feelings.

Closure

Group de-roles from any part they have played by taking off the imaginary cloak of the character and saying 'I'm not _____ I am (their own name)'.

Game: to re-establish the group identity

The whole group moves around the room. At a given signal everyone stops and closes their eyes and when a person's name is mentioned points to where in the room they think that person is. Everyone is given a turn at being mentioned.

Visualisation and relaxation

N.B. Care must be taken to keep the visualisation fairly short and light. Words used must always conjure up the positive and safe. Words such as 'dark' and 'steep' should be avoided.

- Ask the children to sit or lie comfortably and listen to their breathing.
- Ask them to allow their out-breath to become longer than the in-breath. (Counting in and out may be useful here.)
- Ask them to imagine that they are somewhere they feel really safe – their own safe place.
- Ask them to really note what is around them in their safe place, what they can see, the colours, smells, sounds and so on.
- Allow them time to be in this place.
- Tell them they can return to this place any time they wish to do so by closing their eyes and concentrating on their breathing.
- Ask them to slowly become aware of the room around them, the sounds, sensations and so on and, when they are ready, to open their eyes. (Give them time to do this slowly.)

Variation: ask them to imagine that they have just done something which they can be really proud of and that they are receiving an award for this.

As long as the suggestions are positive and language evoking the higher conscious instead of the subconscious is used, there may be many different variants for a visualisation exercise. The aim is to leave the children feeling positive, empowered and relaxed.

Appendix A

Index of Issues and Supporting Exercises and Activities

N.B. These exercises and activities may address more than one issue. Chapter 5 gives ideas for use of fairy tales, myths and legends with various issues.

Issue	Supporting exercise or activity	Reference	Page
Self-esteem-building	Family and friends	The Pointed Diamond	55
	Hero identification	The Magic Book	25
	The shield	The Baby Alien	45
	Various	The Baby Tadpole	38
	Various	The Indian Girl	48
Socially inappropriate behaviour	Various	The Alien Mr Giraffe	32
(Moral dilemmas)	Dick Whittington	The Pointed Diamond	55
(Learnt behaviour)	Role awareness	The Queen Who Shouted	60
	Positive and negative roles	The Queen Who Shouted	60
	Scenarios	The Queen Who Shouted	60
Speech defects	Various	The Indian Girl	48
Trust-building	Trustline	Johnny's stories	41
	Contracts	Through the Wall	68

Appendix B

Useful Sources and Suggested Training

Books

Apuleius, L. (1976) *The Golden Ass*. Harmondsworth: Penguin.

Benson, J. F. (1995) *Working More Creatively With Groups*. London: Routledge.

Brandes, D. (1982) *Gamesters' Handbook Two*. Cheltenham: Stanley Thornes.

Brandes, D. and H. Phillips, (1977) *Gamesters' Handbook*. Cheltenham: Stanley Thornes.

Ehrlich, A. (1985) *The Walker Book of Fairytales*. New York: Random House.

Erikson, E. H. (1959) *Identity and the Life Cycle*, Psychological Issues Monograph. New York: International Universities Press.

Estes, C. P. (1992) *Women Who Run With The Wolves*. London: Rider.

Jennings, S. (1986) *Creative Drama in Group Work*. Bicester: Winslow Press.

Miller, P. H. (1983) *Theories of Developmental Psychology*. New York: W.H. Freeman & Co.

Murdock, M. (1987) *Spinning Inward: Using Guided Imagery with Children for Learning, Creativity and Relaxation*. Boston, Mass. and London: Shambala.

Philip, N. (1995) *The Illustrated Book of Myths*. London: Dorling Kindersley.

Training

For more information on dramatherapy and dramatherapy training visit the website of the British Association of Dramatherapists on http://www.badth.org.uk or write to

The British Association of Dramatherapists
41 Broomhouse Lane
Hurlingham Park
London SW6 3DP

Training in dramatherapy is currently offered at:

- The University of Derby
  Telephone: 01332 592040
- St Loye's School of Health Studies, Exeter
  Telephone: 01392 219774
- The University of Surrey
  Tel: 020 8392 3807
- Manchester University
  Telephone: 01484 428427

- Sesame: The Central School of Speech and Drama
  Telephone: 020 77228183

Suggested training for teaching assistants, teachers and learning mentors who may be delivering structured pastoral or care programmes and wish to use the supporting exercises and activities in this book:

In Service or LEA Training, or both, in the following:

- Counselling
- Child protection
- Listening skills
- Developmental group work
- Solution-focused brief therapy or communication.

Bibliography and References

Axline, V. (1984) *Dibs in Search of Self*. London: Penguin.

Axline, V. (1989) *Play Therapy*. Edinburgh: Churchill Livingstone Publishers.

Benson, J. F. (1995) *Working more Creatively with Groups*. London: Routledge.

Bettelheim, B. (1991) *The Uses of Enchantment*. London: Penguin.

Bowlby, J. (1969) *Attachment and Loss* Volume 1. London: Hogarth Press.

Brun, B., Pederson, E. W. and Runberg, M. (1993) *Symbols of the Soul: Therapy and Guidance Through Fairy Tales*. London: Jessica Kingsley Publishers.

Casson, J. (1998) 'Right/Left Brain and Dramatherapy'. *Dramatherapy Journal* 20 spring: 14.

Emunah, R. (1995) 'From Adolescent Trauma to Adolescent Drama', in S. Jennings (ed.) *Dramatherapy with Children and Adolescents*. London: Routledge.

Gersie, A. (1991) *Storymaking in Bereavement: Dragons Fight in the Meadow*. London: Jessica Kingsley Publishers.

Gersie, A. (1992) *Earth Tales*. London: Green Print.

Haslam, M. (1990) *Psychiatry*. Oxford: Butterworth-Heinemann Ltd.

Jennings, S. (1990) 'Theatre art. The heart of dramatherapy', Keynote presented at the Annual Conference of the British Association of Dramatherapists.

Jennings, S. (ed.) (1995) *Dramatherapy with Children and Adolescents*. London: Routledge.

Jennings, S., Cattanach, A., Mitchell, S., Chesner, A. and Meldrum, B. (1994) *The Handbook of Dramatherapy*. London and New York: Routledge.

Landy, R. (1993) *Persona and Performance. The Meaning of Role in Dramatherapy and Everyday Life*. London: Jessica Kingsley Publishers.

Langley, D. (1995/6) 'An Interview with Peter Slade'. *Dramatherapy Journal* 17, winter: 2.

Mann, S. (1996) 'Metaphor, symbol and the healing process in dramatherapy'. *Dramatherapy Journal* 18, summer: 2.

Miller, P. (1983) *Theories of Developmental Psychology*. New York: W. H. Freeman and Company.

Piaget, J. (1970) 'Piaget's theory', in P. H. Mussen (ed.) *Carmichael's Manual of Child Psychology*, Volume 1. New York: John Wiley.

Radmall, B. (1995) 'The use of role play in dramatherapy'. *Dramatherapy Journal* 17, summer: 13.

Whitmont, E. C. (1991) *The Symbolic Quest. Basic Concepts of Analytical Psychology*. Princeton, NJ: Princeton University Press.

Winnicott, D. W. (1965) *The Maturational Processes and the Facilitating Environment*. London: Hogarth Press.

Winnicott, D. W. (1971) *Playing and Reality*. Harmondsworth: Penguin.

Index

Note: Entries in *italics* denote children's stories